Straightening My Crown

CONQUERING MY ROYAL MISTAKES

MACKENZIE DOUTHIT McKEE

with Julie Markussen

POST HILL PRESS

A POST HILL PRESS BOOK
ISBN: 978-1-64293-984-2
ISBN (eBook): 978-1-64293-985-9

Straightening My Crown:
Conquering My Royal Mistakes
© 2021 by Mackenzie Douthit McKee
All Rights Reserved

Cover Photo by Whitney Osborn

This is a work of nonfiction. All people, locations, events, and situations are portrayed to the best of the author's memory.

Post Hill Press
New York • Nashville
posthillpress.com

Published in the United States of America
1 2 3 4 5 6 7 8 9 10

To my mom, thank you for walking this earth as a perfect example of love, grace, passion, hope, and integrity. Everything I am today is because of the life lessons you taught me and the examples you set.

To my dad, thank you for showing me what being truly loved looks like. You are so full of strength, and it amazes me daily. You love your wife and kids more than any man I know. You are my superhero.

To my siblings, Whitney, Kaylee, Zeke, and Mike, who are full of grace and love.

To my grandma Jayne, who traveled the country to watch me compete and has always been a huge cheerleader in my life.

To Cayla for walking through every season of life with me.

To my kids, Gannon, Jaxie, and Broncs, for being my blessings and saving grace.

And to Josh, for being my best friend.

CONTENTS

INTRODUCTION

Trust in the Lord with all your heart and lean not on
your own understanding. In all your ways submit
to him, and he will make your paths straight.
Proverbs 3: 5–6

When I was first approached about writing this book, I had major reservations. I didn't know if I was ready to go through with it
while taking care of my three kids, making an out-of-state move,
and juggling two businesses of my own. Where could I possibly
find the time to write a book?

Not only was time an issue, but I was also figuring out how
to crawl out of a dark place. I was depressed and anxious, and
everything was catching up to me at the same time. My mom's
death and some very public marital issues were splashed across
the internet and tabloids, and it was all playing out on TV. I
couldn't see the light at the end because I was stuck smack dab in
the middle of that deep tunnel. Everyone had an opinion about
me, my life, and the choices I had made, and they all seemed to
believe every lie that was on the internet about me.

Ever since I can remember, I seem to make the wrong choices
in life before learning to make better ones. Being diagnosed
with ADHD (attention deficit hyperactivity disorder) and type 1

diabetes only complicated things more. However, I come from a very levelheaded, amazing family. They were loved and respected by everyone around them, and were active members of our community and church. My siblings saved themselves for marriage, while I got pregnant at sixteen. Even though it was hard to compare myself to them, I was thankful for the good examples they set for me, and no matter what, I knew they always had my back. I truly come from an amazing family.

I was also worried that with all my recent personal turmoil, my story wouldn't have a happy ending, and I felt that my readers (and I) deserved a happy ending.

I've never learned things the easy way, and I often think about how my mom said I was just "wired differently" than my siblings. She made me realize, too, that being different is nothing to be ashamed of. She used to tell me that it was okay to stumble and fall now and then as long as I got back up. And if my crown falls off in the process, I need to pick it up, straighten it, and stand a little taller next time. Every time it slips and falls, it holds more value as I fix it and put it back on. My mom loved all kinds of women's empowerment quotes, and she would frequently tell my sisters and me to keep our chins up so our crowns wouldn't fall off. She wanted us to know our true worth and never be ashamed of who we are. There have been countless times my crown has been crooked, and it's still a little crooked right now. Nobody's perfect, and we are all more alike than we know. But if I can learn from and conquer my mistakes (and I've made some *royal* ones, believe me), anyone can. You might even notice that my cover photo is far from perfect, but it was important for me to show myself as I truly am—with minimal makeup and straightening my crown while a wave washes over me. My sister Whitney is a photographer, and she was willing (at eight months pregnant!) to get into the freezing water with me to catch that perfectly imperfect *(unretouched)* shot. I love her and the photo she captured for showing the real me.

I've experienced amazing growth throughout my life. I could wait forever for the "right time" to write a book, but then it occurred to me that most of the important events in my life didn't happen at what most people would call the "right time." But I also know my ups and downs have taught me to persevere and stay strong, and most importantly, they've taught me who I am.

I hope that sharing my mistakes and what I've learned might help others straighten their crowns too. We all just have to believe in ourselves and trust that our paths may be a little different from the paths of others and that everything will happen according to God's plan. His plan isn't always the same as our own, but it is far bigger and better than anything we could ever imagine. It's up to us to be willing to stop, listen, and seek what His plan has in store for us. Since I always learn the hard way, maybe this *was* the perfect time to tell my story. After all, I'd have to straighten my own crown first before I could help others straighten theirs.

Even though my relationship with God is an important part of who I am and what I believe, and I talk a lot about His love in this book, I want people to know that I never judge others for having beliefs that differ from my own. His grace is just too influential to who I am to ignore that part of my life. The Bible verses I've included have helped me through tough times, so I wanted to share them with others.

And about that happy ending…it might not arrive at the perfect time or in the easiest way, but I know my happy ending is coming. I'm forging ahead on whatever path I need to take to get there, and I'm ready to face any challenges headfirst with my crown held high.

Chapter 1

THE TOUGH TALK

*But to each one of us grace has been
given as Christ apportioned it.*
Ephesians 4:7

was sitting in my room after school, waiting for my mom to get home. I'd just put the finishing touches on redecorating my walls with the latest posters from my favorite celebrity magazines. Like most sixteen-year-olds, I loved plastering the walls of my bedroom from top to bottom with posters of actors and actresses and music stars to jazz up my room and make me feel cool. One thing I always knew I got from my mom was my love for interior decorating. And since my house was where all my cheerleader friends hung out after school and had sleepovers, I had to make sure my bedroom always looked perfect. But this particular day, it was just me, and I knew for sure that although Beyoncé and Hilary Duff were staring back at me from the wall, they certainly weren't going to back me up when I told my mom the secret I was hiding. I had a feeling this might not go well. I heard the doorknob click as she came into my room. This was it. I couldn't hold anything back now. My decision had already been made.

"Mom, sit down. I have to talk to you," I said, nervously tapping my feet. I've always had so much energy that it is impossible for me to sit still—and that was especially true at that moment. As my mom sat down on my bed beside me, I told myself to take a deep breath and just let it out. Now was the time to speak. She was a very wise, involved mom and could always read me like a book, so I could tell by the look on her face that she knew it wasn't going to be good.

"Mom, I'm pregnant."

For a few seconds, my mom just stared at me. Her posture slumped, and she seemed to melt into the bed. She said nothing. I was desperate to hear her say something—*anything*. But she didn't. Not right away. I'm sure it was only a moment of silence, but it seemed like an eternity. She just stood up and stared at my new posters.

My mom would *always* think about things before she did them, and it was so rare to see my mom snap that I didn't expect her to snap now. I had never even heard her swear. The closest she ever got to losing her temper happened one time in middle school. She said the word "freaking" when she was dropping me off at a school dance and had her final straw of my back-talking. It's the worst word I'd ever heard her say. She said, "You're being freaking pathetic," as I got out of the car. It took her days to forgive herself for saying that to me, even when I assured her that my friends' moms cussed all the time. And now, even though the blank look on her face showed she was clearly in shock, I was positive that she would keep calm. Boy, was I wrong.

Standing up slowly, she turned her gaze to my poster wall. Britney Spears smiling down at her seemed to set her off. She started ripping my posters off the wall and throwing them on the ground. I had never seen her this infuriated before. She didn't stop until every single one was crumpled on my bedroom floor. She walked out of the room, and in walked my dad. I knew she hadn't told him, so it would be up to me to share the news with my precious, gentle, loving father. To this day, it's the hardest thing I've ever had to tell him. Upon hearing my confession, we sat together crying. Finally, after a few hours with my dad, my mom came back into my room. When she regained her composure, she started asking questions.

"Mackenzie, where did I go wrong? I've had four kids and raised you all the same way. How did this happen?"

I glanced over my shoulder and saw my reflection in the mirror. As I exhaled the breath I had been holding, I could feel the hot sensation of shame spreading throughout my body. I knew I had failed my mom—just like I had failed myself as a small child when I couldn't protect myself from trouble. Now I was failing as a teenager and feeling my dreams slip through my fingers. My mom and I had spent my whole childhood since the age of four traveling all around the country for all-star cheer lessons and competitions. My family didn't have much money, and she had sacrificed so much for me because she just knew I was going somewhere with my life. And here I was. I had ruined everything.

Not waiting for any answers, my mom walked abruptly out of my room. Unsettled by her display of rage, I grabbed a few things and went to my boyfriend's house to escape the pain at home. Within an hour, she ended up texting me. "Mackenzie, I'm sorry. It was wrong for me to act that way. I will always love you no matter what." I let out a sigh of relief, knowing that she seemed to be back on my side. But I still couldn't figure out how to slow my heart rate down. I swear I could see my heart pumping out of my chest. I went back home and went to bed, knowing there would be plenty more to figure out the next day.

All night, I tried to make sense of my mom's reaction. Maybe she ripped my posters because they were a symbol of how I had always tried to fit in with the popular crowd. She already knew that I had lost my virginity not long before and had also warned me about some of the friends I was choosing to hang around. Then one of those "friends" ratted me out to my mom—telling her that I was sleeping with my then-boyfriend. Looking for any sign that my friend was right, my mom went digging in my dresser drawers and found the birth control pills I had gotten by sneaking behind her back. When I got home from school on the day she found them, she said one of the most hurtful things that she'd ever said to me: "You're not my baby girl anymore." It crushed me.

My mom forbade me from staying on birth control after she found out I was sexually active because, in her mind, that was just giving me permission to have more sex. I guess she just trusted that I wouldn't sleep with my next boyfriend either because she never brought up the topic and must have thought that I had learned my lesson when she caught me before.

After that, I started rebelling. It is this season of life I wish I could go back and redo. I would listen to and respect my mom more and see that she just wanted what was best for me. Back then, I would constantly talk back to my mom, and some days when I was told no, I would scream, punch holes in the wall, and destroy my room. My siblings thought I was a spoiled brat, and they were angry at the way I was treating our mom. It's still a joke in my family that I got more spankings in one day than the other three of them put together ever did during their entire childhoods. I had anger problems, and my siblings didn't understand how I became the bad kid.

I never understood why my parents didn't have a conversation with me about pregnancy or sex before marriage because they had experienced both as teenagers. One big difference is that my dad married my mom right away when they found out she was pregnant, and he was the only man she had ever been with (or ever would be with). When they were teens, it was much more common to get married young and stay together. I also think that my mom understood that love stories like theirs were rare and special. She inspired my dad to come to God, and he loved her unconditionally for it. God seemed to have made my parents for each other, and I always thought a man would love me as my dad loved my mom. Through a lot of mistakes, I learned the hard way that not all men are like my dad.

In retrospect, my mom must have seen a lot of herself in me. I believe that, right then, she was remembering how hard it was to tell her own parents about her pregnancy. Her parents (my grandparents) had been very involved in the church, and she, too, felt like she had failed them at that time in her life. As active leaders in the church, my grandparents knew this would cause heartache and gossip for their family, and they were right. People were cruel and judgmental, and after going through the pain of having others talk behind her back, there was no way my mom wanted one of her children to experience that too.

Getting pregnant at sixteen wasn't something I could blame on the way my mom raised me, though. Some damaging things had happened to me as a small child that ruined my self-esteem and must have contributed to the poor decisions I was making. I wasn't angry with *her* for those awful things. I had kept them secret for years, and she had no idea they had even happened. How was she supposed to know? I didn't even understand the extent of what had happened and how it had affected me until later in life. No, I thought that everything that had gotten me here was because I was different and doomed—unlike my siblings, who didn't make the kind of mistakes I did. Like my mom, I couldn't understand why I was the only one to suffer from my bad choices, but I knew, in the end, I only had myself to blame.

The next morning, my mom came into my room to talk. Reaching out to grab my hand, she still had tears in her eyes. I could tell that she, too, had not slept all night. I was only a few walls away from her, but that night, I felt like I was in another country. She was my comfort any time I was broken, and I just wanted to talk to her. "We're going to do this. We're going to have this baby, Mickey," she said.

That was the day I was certain that things would never be the same for either of us.

Crowning Achievement:

God gave my mom a huge gift of grace. I know it was not easy for her to forgive me and face the world with a sixteen-year-old pregnant daughter, but she was a true example of Christ.

Chapter 2

NOT ACCORDING TO PLAN

For I know the plans I have for you, declares
the Lord, plans to prosper you and not to harm
you, plans to give you hope and future.
Jeremiah 19:11

come from Miami, but not the one with the pastel colors, beaches, flamingos, and vibrant nightlife in Florida. No, I am from the Miami (pronounced *"My-am-uh"*) in the far northeast corner of Oklahoma. The whole town is only ten square miles and has a population under fourteen thousand. Miami was once a booming mining town in the mid-1800s, situated on a stretch of historic Route 66 not too far away from the Missouri and Kansas borders. But now it's known more for its casinos and the fact that about 25 percent of its residents live in poverty—many with drug and gambling problems.

My parents, Brad and Angie Douthit, were also born in the same area, my dad being just one town over in Wyandotte, Oklahoma. Their love story started in first grade when they rode the same bus to school. My dad remembers being so jealous of my mom's friend, who not only got to sit next to her on the bus but also got to share my mom's candy. No matter how nice he was to them, they wouldn't share their candy with him, and he thought they were stuck up for not giving him some. Still, all through elementary and middle school, my dad kept trying (without luck) to catch my mom's eye.

At fifteen, he realized he was in love with her, and somehow, he convinced my mom to go on a real date. But despite his changing my mom's feelings for him, my mom's parents now were the ones who had nothing good to say about him. He just wasn't the type of boy they wanted their daughter to come home with—ever. My dad loved to party and drink with his friends, which didn't win him any points with my grandparents. When my mom realized how wild he was, she didn't want to put up with his partying lifestyle either and broke up with him. He dealt with this like a lot of young boys would—by getting even more drunk with friends every night and even showing up at her parents' doorstep. (If you knew my mother's parents, you would know that is *not* a good idea.) He was so miserable without her. He *had* to have his precious Angie back. Somehow, he must have worn her down because they rekindled, and from then on, they were inseparable. She was able to lead my dad to God, and she gave him a lot of grace for the mistakes he made.

When she got pregnant at eighteen, she broke the news to her parents that she and the guy they weren't crazy about were going to be parents. They were horrified that their daughter would now be the talk of the town as an unwed mother. My mom, they believed, had fallen for this untamed guy who had won her over. And she was now carrying his child.

My dad, however, *knew* he was going to marry my mom. As a young teenager, he told her that his love for her was forever. In fact, *he* was the one who talked my mom into marrying him. She borrowed a friend's dress, and they quickly planned a twenty-dollar wedding with their friends and family. It was a perfect celebration of love in their eyes.

After the ceremony, my dad barely had enough money in his wallet to take my mom to a special honeymoon dinner at Red Lobster. Throughout their thirty-four-year-long marriage, Red Lobster remained their favorite date spot.

The issue of where they would live as a newlywed couple was quickly solved by my dad's father. He had forty acres with a trailer house on it, and he let them live there as long as they agreed to help manage his farm. Soon after they moved to the farm, my oldest sister Whitney was born. While living in the trailer, my parents were broke, but my dad said that my mom never complained. That's easy to believe because I hardly ever heard her complain during the twenty-five years of my life that I knew her. Being so poor, she would often buy just one bag of potatoes that she made go a long way by teaching herself to make different dishes. Within two years of married life, they were pregnant again with my sister Kaylee.

But my mom always had a huge heart, and she didn't want to stop at just two children. In their early twenties, after my two sisters were born, my parents decided that they wanted to be foster parents. My mom always had a heart for kids who needed a better home, so they began to pray about it, and God answered.

After months of waiting, my mom's father called her. He worked for child welfare, and he had wonderful news for them. There was a boy who would be perfect for my parents. But there was one little catch. The "boy" was a thirty-four-year-old man with Down syndrome named Mike. His mother had just died, and since he was an only child, he had no one to take care of him. He desperately wanted a family to which he could belong, but my parents wondered if it would be too difficult to adopt someone older than they were. My mom, however, had such a huge and loving heart, and she couldn't get Mike off her mind.

The facility where Mike was staying allowed him to visit my family for the weekend, and my mom instantly knew that he should be a part of our family. It took some convincing to get my dad on board, as he was absolutely terrified to take on a grown man with disabilities. He and my mom were barely adults themselves, and they were barely making ends meet and living in a trailer with two small girls. But my mom never questioned God's plan, and she assured my dad that Mike was destined to be a part of our family.

Even though it wasn't the image they had in their heads, instead of being worried about the situation, my parents were open-minded and trusted God. My mom prayed for guidance, saying, "Well, God, this certainly wasn't my plan, but it's Your plan. And Your plan has got to be better than my plan!" With that, they moved forward with their plan to adopt Mike.

They began to worry, though, that their trailer wasn't big enough for their growing family, but they didn't have money to buy a larger home. That's when pure luck struck. Mike's mom had left her house to him in her will, so now my parents and sisters could move in and live there with Mike. Having never been able to afford their own house, my parents wondered what they could have possibly done for God to give them this incredible opportunity. They immediately began building on another master suite so Mike would have a room and space to himself. When the house was ready, my family moved in, with my sisters sharing one room, and my parents, the other.

Life with Mike was a blessing, and my parents felt so much satisfaction from their decision to adopt him. He was sweet, loving, and extremely funny. Humor just came naturally to him. He was hilarious, and he enjoyed making people laugh.

One of Mike's favorite things was to be around people. At church, he eagerly listened and accepted God's word. He loved praising and worshipping God to the point that he started speaking loudly in tongues whenever he went to church. No one minded because everyone in the church was crazy about him! Even if they didn't like any of the rest of my family, they loved Mike, and Mike loved everyone back. He absolutely adored kids, so he would sometimes go to the elementary school where my dad worked, and while my dad was cleaning and doing his custodial duties around the school, little kids would come up to Mike to say hi and talk to him. To Mike, this was his version of Heaven.

Even though Mike loved my whole family, he was obsessed with my dad, who became his hero. He even had a nickname for my dad—"Lambie Pie." We had no idea where he came up with that nickname, and I'm not sure my dad really liked it, but "Lambie Pie" he was. My dad was still pretty young at this time, and he had a big group of friends with whom he'd play softball. Of course, Mike was always there to watch and cheer him on. I can only imagine my dad's embarrassment when his friends laughed at him while Mike was yelling, "There he is! That's my Lambie Pie! Go, Lambie Pie! You're so cute!" My dad would just put his face in his hands while everyone else enjoyed Mike's enthusiasm.

And as for my mom, Mike would likely not have had such a good life after his biological mom had passed if it hadn't been for her. She loved him without reservation and let him be himself. He loved her for it and thought she was the most beautiful woman in the world, calling her "Farrah Fawcett" after his favorite TV star. My mom always went out of her way to help Mike feel like he belonged, even letting him play "pin the tail on the elephant" instead of a donkey at birthday parties because he was such a die-hard Republican. She never told him what to believe or think, and she let him live his life how he wanted.

Within two years of adopting Mike, my brother Zeke was born, and he was yet another happy, easygoing kid to raise, aside from some scary illnesses he went through as a baby. My mom still felt our home had room for at least one more child to love, though. She was one of those moms who could handle several kids with no stress. Pregnancy was actually enjoyable to her, and parenting came naturally too. My parents already had two girls, one boy, and one man, and they wanted to complete their perfect pattern with one more child they assumed would be another boy. His name would be Hunter, and he would grow to be best friends with his older brother—just like his two older sisters were best friends. And then...*surprise!* Nineteen months later, I was born.

Not expecting a girl, my parents didn't even have a name picked out for me until after I was born. They told me different stories on how they came up with "Mackenzie." My mom's version is that she liked the name Mackenzie, and while she was reading a book about Walt Disney, it dawned on her that "Mickey" would be a cute nickname for Mackenzie. My dad, on the other hand, tells a story of demanding that my mother drive him to McDonald's for a Big Mac while she was in labor on the way to the hospital. He insists that must have been the inspiration for Mackenzie. Funny enough, my friends in school always called me "Big Mac" as a nickname without knowing this story, and many of my newer friends just call me "Mac." My family still calls me "Mickey" to this day. Personally, I've always liked calling myself "Kenzie," but at work, I introduce myself as "Coach Mac." I like to believe that I have so many nicknames because I'm multifaceted and there's more to me than meets the eye. Each name helps me sparkle from a different angle.

I was the baby who screamed and screamed, and if I wasn't screaming, I was nursing. I was always told I came out screaming and never stopped. When I was born, the doctors were set to tie my mom's tubes, but she wasn't sure she was ready to be done yet. However, after three solid months of no sleep, my mom knew she was done having children. She always told me, "There's a reason you were my last—you are a handful!" One day, my dad came home from work, and without telling him where they were going, she whisked him into her minivan. He saw in her eyes that she was exhausted to no end and didn't ask questions about where they were going. The next thing you know, they were at the doctor's office, scheduling him for a vasectomy.

Even though she was through having kids, my mom didn't want me to grow up since I was the last one. She wanted to baby me and keep me little for as long as possible, which made it easy for me to get away with murder. I could scream and throw fits, and my mom couldn't tell me no. My siblings saw this and deemed me a strong-willed spoiled brat. And I don't blame them.

Even though I wasn't the boy my parents had planned, my brother and I were close. To fit in with Zeke, I learned to play rough. My blonde hair was always tangled in snarls, and my face was constantly dirty from playing outside. Thankfully, my mom was easygoing about having a lively girl. If I went to church without shoes (which I did several times), she didn't care. Life was too short in her eyes to stress over silly shoes. She refused to subscribe to the stereotype that girls had to wear frilly dresses and pink bows. She let me be me, whoever I was.

Over the years, I've spent a lot of time looking in the mirror and wondering why I'm not more like my siblings. I'm slowly beginning to accept my differences and learn that it's okay to take your own path in life. My mom taught me that things won't always go according to our plan, but they always go according to *God's* plan. I had to dig deep to find out the lessons that He wanted me to learn.

Crowning Achievement:

I love this part of my family story because it shows that our life doesn't always line up with the vision in our heads, but following God's plan for us will lead to hope. Taking on Mike was not easy. It took a lot of patience and came with unexpected challenges and uncertainty. But it was a huge blessing in the end.

Chapter 3

HAPPY WITH WHAT WE HAD

I can do all things through Christ who strengthens me.
Philippians 4:13

Always jumping, running, and playing, I became obsessed with gymnastics at the age of four after seeing it on TV. I immediately knew that I wanted to be a gymnast, and no one could stop me. Unfortunately, since my family was so tight on money, my mom explained to me that gymnastic lessons were extremely expensive. However, she said that if I could teach myself a back handspring, she would find a way to pay for them. I'm sure she thought there was no way that a four-year-old was going to learn a backflip on her own, but I was set to prove her wrong. Somehow, I would learn.

My mom should have known what she was getting herself into, since I was so feisty and fearless. She had recently taught me how to ride a bike, and after seeing my older siblings ride, I demanded that she take off my training wheels too. As everyone was inside living life, I was outside alone and wouldn't sleep or eat until I could ride my bike without those training wheels. No one would dare stand in the way or show me how. I would learn on my own, and I did. My mom just stood back, laughed, and shook her head when she saw me.

So, when it came to learning a backflip, I wore myself out for three days trying. Even at this young age, I wasn't scared of getting hurt, and I spent hours flipping my body and falling all over the lawn and the house. Then it dawned on me—my parents had a waterbed! That would be the *perfect* place to create a soft landing!

Excitedly, I jumped onto the waterbed and gave it all I had, flinging my legs over my head. A perfect backflip! But since no one saw it but me, I would have to practice until I could do it outside and prove it to my mom. Again and again, I flipped on the water bed until...*pop!* The waterbed mattress broke, and water started flooding my parents' bedroom, but I knew that doing a backflip on a waterbed wasn't going to impress my mom—especially when I had already ruined the bed and the carpet. I would just have to learn a backflip on solid ground.

Shortly after the waterbed catastrophe, I finally landed my flip on the front lawn. I just told myself that I would go for it, and just like that, I somehow pulled it off! I ran into the kitchen where my mom was fixing a big pot of vegetable and deer steak stew (from one my dad had shot for us) and screamed at the top of my lungs, "I did it! I did it! You have to come see!"

She rushed outside, watched, and just smiled and said, "Oh, my! Mackenzie has done it again." I remember the day I overheard her calling the local tumbling gym on our house phone to get me in like it was yesterday.

At this point, she was certain that I would be stubborn and determined for life. My personality traits might make this life quite a journey for me, but she assured me that my drive and grit would take me places if I used them productively. When she told me that she would always be there to help and cheer me on no matter what, I believed her. And she did stand by me—often when no one else would.

Let's say that my mom wasn't too happy about the bed, but she had to hand it to me—I learned a backflip, and she would now have to find a way to get me those lessons. Most children have to start in the gym and be taught their first flips, but I walked in being the one who taught herself. I honestly didn't know how much we struggled financially until much later in life, and now, I am amazed at how we ever survived. When I was in second grade, my mom lost the daycare she owned due to one unfortunately selfish human who made up lies that forced her to close, and she hadn't found another job. My dad was making minimum wage as a custodian at my elementary school. We were barely getting by, yet somehow, my parents never let us kids know that we were struggling. My mom said that while she may be short on money, she had a mansion waiting for her in Heaven because she tithed and gave money to the church no matter how horribly we struggled. She always told us to "cast all your cares on God" while she was hiding her worries about the survival of our family. My family never got to go on yearly trips to places like Disneyland or the beach or have fancy dinners, and the only real family trip they ever took was one I didn't get to enjoy—it was over twenty-five years ago while my mom was pregnant with me!

One thing that financially struggling taught me was that if I want something badly enough, I'd have to work hard and sometimes go to extremes to make it happen. I was determined and thrifty, and I learned how to stretch a dime like my mom stretched that bag of potatoes. A perfect example of this happened every year at Christmas. At the beginning of the year, my mom would start saving so she could give us all a good holiday. She knew that my siblings and I loved gum, and Christmas was the only time all year that my mom bought it for us. She loaded up our Christmas stockings and filled them to the brim with candy and gum. On Christmas morning, while my sisters and brother were busy chomping away their gum stashes, I would get out a piece of paper and a calculator and work out how many pieces of gum I could chew each week to make it last until next Christmas. And you know what? I made it last every year! I was a mess and the most difficult child of the bunch, but it was no secret I could make anything happen that I set my mind to. Everyone knew I already had an eye for business at a young age. It just came naturally.

Somehow, my mom found the money to enroll me in gymnastics and cheer lessons. There were no gyms or cheer coaches in our hometown, Miami, so my mom found a gym just across the Oklahoma border in Joplin, Missouri. She drove me to that gym three days a week, and I spent so much time in the car with my mom and in the gym as she cheered me on. I grew up in that gym, and all the time together brought my mom and me closer. My grandma would often go along to my competitions, and she was so proud of me and loved being so involved in her grandchildren's lives. Before I'd compete, she'd say, "Go get 'em, tiger," and my mom would say, "Remember, Sis, you can do ALL things through Christ who strengthens you." Every time she said it, I let it soak in. All of us kids knew Philippians 4:13 at a young age.

When taking me to the gym, my mom was paying turnpike and gas fees, as well as laying down a lot of cash for my lessons. Additionally, she and my grandma traveled a lot for my competitions, where my mom also had to pay registration fees for me to compete and spend serious money for the hotels we stayed in and the expensive competition leotards I had to wear. I know now that my parents often argued about the money spent on my tumbling fixation, but they never let me hear it. And on those days when I was being a brat and rude to my mom, my dad told her that she should take gymnastics and cheer away from me, but she refused. She said that they needed to show me grace instead of punishment. I may have been a hard kid to raise, but the work I put into my skills was always above and beyond. If I wasn't the top tumbler and flyer in the gym, I would quickly figure out how to become the best. I know that all-star cheer saved me in life.

And remember all that time we spent in the car? My mom drove the crappiest car with a bad transmission. The windows wouldn't even roll down. If we were driving past a group of cute boys, I would get so embarrassed, but my mom would just laugh and encourage me not to take things so seriously. We were poor at this time of life, but we didn't know it because my mom made life so fun. But come to think of it, in the long run, it might have been less expensive to just get me those lessons in the beginning, because now she was stuck paying for them *and* a new bed!

Crowning Achievement:

We are all only human, and no one is perfect. We were all given different gifts and talents, strengths and weaknesses, and that is what makes the world so beautiful. When I say I am a child of God, I mean I am so weak and such a sinner that I need him to strengthen me. Throughout life, whether I've needed emotional or physical strength, I've clung tightly to Philippians 4:13—just like my mother taught me.

Chapter 4

INNOCENCE LOST

*Repay no one evil for evil, but give thought to do what is
honorable in the sight of all. If possible, so far as it depends
on you, live peaceably with all. Beloved, never avenge
yourselves, but leave it to the wrath of God, for it is written,
"Vengeance is mine, I will repay," says the Lord.*
Romans 12:17–19

While my brothers and sisters clung to my mom, I
was more of a wanderer. As a wild, independent
child, I was always on the move. I would disappear
at church, and no one knew where I was. I was left home alone
more than once because my parents couldn't find me. And even
one time, when I was a toddler, my parents looked all over the
house and were convinced I'd been kidnaped. After scouring

the neighborhood and our house, they finally found me—asleep under my crib.

As a little girl, I didn't ever watch TV or sit down quietly, thanks to my ADHD. I was outside the minute school was out, and my dream was to someday own a farm where I could run around freely with pigs, horses...you name it. Another way I'm not like my siblings is that I have always had a love for animals, while my sisters just think they poop and they're gross. Even my brother isn't a huge fan of having pets. They all like other people's animals, but they don't want their own, unlike me. They wanted to be clean, but if I wasn't looking for or playing with animals as a kid, I was on all fours with my friends, pretending to be an animal.

Anyone who knows me well knows that I've always been a true extrovert who wants nothing more than to be around people. Between the smaller kids at my mom's daycare and my older siblings' friends, I was rarely around kids my own age. Because I was half the size of kids my own age and less mature, most people I met thought I was much younger than I actually was. My mom always had a joke she would tell about how little I was. She'd point at me and say, "I feed and water, but it doesn't grow!" Being so tiny and scrawny, older kids often saw me as someone they could easily take advantage of and manipulate, and wanting so desperately to have friends and be liked, I usually complied so I could fit in.

When I was around four years of age, there was a boy at the daycare my mom ran in her house who was about eight years older than I was. We often played together, and one day, he told me we were going to play a new game where we would pretend to be dogs. I loved games and dogs, so naturally, I was excited.

We began imagining that we were puppies, and he told me I would have a special role to play. I was going to be the mommy dog, and he would be the daddy dog. "Mommy dogs," he explained, "didn't wear pants," and he pulled me into the closet and shut the door where no one could find us. I was the mommy dog, and I had to do "puppy things" as all mommy dogs do. The boy did inappropriate things, and this happened a few times. I was confused, but I played along since I wanted so desperately to be liked.

Another time when I was a small child, I was staying the night at the house of someone my mom trusted, and she had an older boy in his early teens. He told me that he wanted to wrestle, and being a rough-and-tumble tomboy, I was ready to throw down. Quickly, I realized this was a different type of wrestling than the one I played with my siblings back home.

Things went in a direction that made me uncomfortable, even though, at that time, I knew nothing. He did it nearly every time I visited. One day, he asked me if I wanted to wrestle, and I told him no. With fire in his eyes, he yelled at me, "No! You *are* going to wrestle with me whether you want to or not." I had never seen him react so angrily and strongly when I refused to play other games, and I wondered why wrestling was so different. After I wouldn't wrestle with him that time, he never wanted to play with me again. I didn't understand why, but I figured that saying no to wrestling must have been the problem, but I didn't know what I could do to make him like me again. I later realized how damaging this is to children. We learn at a young age that people will throw us away if we stand our ground. It also ruins a child's self-esteem, and later in life, that grown child has difficulty seeing where this loss came from.

I didn't even realize that the behavior in which I had participated with these two boys was "bad" until I was in fifth grade when my friend and I were staying at a fancy hotel with her mom. We were left alone in the room while her mom went to a party, telling us she would be back at midnight. As soon as she left, we turned on the TV, and the first thing we saw was porn. Neither of us had ever seen anything like that. In fact, we didn't know that sex even existed. What we saw on TV seemed weird and gross to us, but out of curiosity, we didn't change the channel.

As the movie went on, I started having flashbacks of the puppy game and wrestling. I felt a sense of extreme discomfort wash over me as I realized that what we were watching was an awful lot like the puppy game and the wrestling that the older boys had convinced me to do when I was younger. Even though my friend and I giggled uncomfortably, what was happening in the movie seemed naughty and wrong. It was something reserved for adults, and certainly not something you should force on someone. *"That's been done to me before,"* I thought to myself in horror. *"I'm not a good human. I'm not as pure as my parents think I am. I'm not innocent. I'm dirty and gross, and that's why they like my siblings more."* I felt like I finally had an answer for being different—I had been ruined.

As time went by, the gravity of what happened to me sunk in. These incidents didn't spoil my entire childhood, since I didn't realize it was wrong until later, but I know it must have shaped my personality and influenced other choices I had made. It was a lot to carry this on my shoulders at such a young age, and I knew if I told, I would be called a liar by the boy's parents and ruin my parents' relationships with good family friends. Adults had never done something terrible like this to me as a child, so in my head, I tried to comfort myself with the thought that the boys who did this to me were just young teens and didn't know any better. Still, I couldn't tell my parents what happened. I couldn't tell anyone. In fact, this is the very first time I've shared these stories publicly. I kept this in for so long, but I felt this was the time to share, because maybe my experiences could help someone else who has gone through something similar.

I would never want someone to pity or feel sorry for me because this happened, especially since I know it sadly happens to so many young girls, and for a lot, if not most of them, their experiences are far worse than mine. According to statistics, many young kids are sexually abused, and I truly believe the numbers are actually more than reported because I'm sure there are many small children who, like me, were afraid to speak up. I was a little girl raised by loving and protective Christian parents, and some way, somehow, it still happened to me, so I know it can happen to anyone, and my heart goes out to all those who have had to endure that kind of pain and suffering. No child should ever have to go through something like that.

Those two boys from my childhood are now grown men who still live around my hometown, and I occasionally bump into them when I'm back in Oklahoma. While I don't believe they are the type of adults who would do something like that to children, I could be wrong. Neither one has ever talked to me about what happened or apologized. Maybe they don't remember it happened, or maybe they believe I was too young to remember. Regardless, I don't think for a second that they live with the knowledge that what they did changed my life forever and contributed to losing my self-respect and lowering expectations for myself. I thought I had lost all my value as a human being. I had been abused. And, again, I asked God, *"Why did you let this happen to me?"* Knowing that He would never give me something

I couldn't handle, I still couldn't see what purpose this harm was serving for me now.

I only wish that I would've understood as a child that it wasn't my fault this happened. Anyone who's gone through this should know that there's no need to carry shame and guilt for something that others did to you. I sometimes wish I would have gotten help sooner instead of bottling this inside and letting the pain come out in sinful behavior. But like I always say, our struggles mold us into the strong people we become. This gave me a lot of grace in how I see others. Instead of wondering why people are hateful, I just know they have pain deep inside of them. When other people knock your crown off your head, you're still going to have to find a way to pick it back up and straighten it, but you should never have to feel embarrassed that someone else caused it to fall off in the first place.

Crowning Achievement:

It is not our job to repay evil with evil. I always had a problem with wanting to pay people back with worse than what they did to me, and it never ended well. God says to leave this up to Him and to go on with our lives in peace. Just as I know I will pay for my sins, others will have to pay for theirs as well. Those who do us wrong have nothing to do with us and everything to do with themselves. The bad things that happen to us *do not* define us. That said, I also believe that we all have the opportunity to come to God and ask for forgiveness when we do others wrong. But we should still make sure to always follow through with truly changing our ways.

Chapter 5

THE "WAY-TOO-SWEET" SIXTEEN

*I have said these things to you, that in me you may
have peace. In the world you will have tribulation.
But take heart, I have overcome the world.*
John 16:33

My sixth-grade year was a tough one. I was struggling in school, and the teachers wanted to hold me back a year. I was also losing weight, and I looked so skinny and tired with sunken eyes. Even my tumbling wasn't as strong as it used to be, and when I was too weak to do the gymnastics at my cheer tryouts, I knew something was off. I craved sugar, but I was losing weight by the hour. I remember sitting in class one day, and the boys who always joked about my hot sisters made a comment about one of my photos of them stuffed in the plastic part of my school binder. Already blossoming into the smart businesswoman that I am, I said, "Wanna buy my sister's school photo for a buck?" Within seconds, I handed over her photo, snatched the dollar bill from the boy, and wasted no time in heading to the candy machine to purchase a giant honey bun with white frosting.

Since I was falling further behind academically, one day my teacher asked me to stay after class. She had noticed, along with three of my other teachers, that I was asking to use the restroom three to four times an hour. "If you keep leaving class all the time, Mackenzie, you're never going to get ahead in this class. I know you're just trying to get out of class to text your boyfriend. I think that the only way you'll learn from this is to serve detention," she said.

I tried to explain to her that I didn't even have a boyfriend to text and that I really was just using the restroom or getting a drink at the water fountain. She didn't believe me and said she would call home to let my parents know about the detention.

Knowing that my mom would take the news better if I prepped her for the phone call, I decided to tell her about the detention as soon as I got home from school. I never misbehaved at school, so this was devastating to have to tell her. As we stood in the kitchen, I swore to her that I wasn't trying to ditch class, but that I really had to use the restroom and go to the drinking fountain. I had been so thirsty lately that it seemed as though I just stood there and gulped up the water for minutes at a time. Upon hearing this, my mom, who had been stirring stew at the stove, just stopped and froze. While I begged her not to ground me, she just put her head in her hands and stared straight ahead. I had no idea why my mom was so distraught over this detention. It wasn't that big of a deal, was it? Still, she just stayed silent and quickly changed the subject. Her reaction was so confusing to me, but I didn't pry. I didn't want to get grounded on top of that detention!

The next day was my sister Kaylee's "sweet sixteen" birthday, and the whole family was going to Applebee's that night to celebrate. We were seated, and I asked the server to bring me a large Diet Dr Pepper. I drank it down fast and ordered another one. And then another one. Before the meal had even been served, I had sucked down four Dr Peppers, and I drank several more during the meal. Even though I was always thirsty lately, the amount I drank at dinner made my family take notice. They seemed a little alarmed that no matter how much I drank, it never quenched my thirst. I noticed my mom eyeing me and being uncharacteristically quiet at the table, as all others just laughed without understanding what was going on. She seemed to be concerned and deep in thought, like she was trying to figure something out.

After dinner, Kaylee wanted to go shopping at the mall, so we all went, but I didn't get to shop much because I had to pee at every new store we entered. When we finally went home, it was time to bring out the chocolate cake my mom had made and sing "Happy Birthday" to Kaylee. After devouring my piece of cake, my mom called me into the kitchen alone. She said that she wanted to do an "experiment" with me. "I'm going to check your blood sugar level," she said, "because I just got this new glucometer. Isn't it cool?" She was not very convincing.

"Wait! No! I don't want to stick that in my finger! It'll hurt... and bleed!" I whined. I was a big drama queen, and everyone knew it. Slowly, out of the corner of my eye, I saw the rest of my family file into the kitchen. Knowing that I was a big baby and sensing the seriousness of the situation, my oldest sister Whitney came up with the idea that we would all take the test. "We can all do it! It'll be a game, Mickey. We'll go first. You'll see—it's not that bad!" Well, since this was going to be a game, and I loved a good family competition, I said okay.

One by one, my siblings lined up to have my mom prick their fingers to check their blood sugar levels, and each of them had the same perfect reading. Now it was my turn. It took them a while to hold me down for this tiny finger prick. I screamed, I kicked, and I wanted to so badly to get out of it. After a tiny finger prick, I exclaimed, "That didn't even hurt!" Looking down, I saw that the glucometer read "HI." No one else's said that. I turned to look at my mom, and instead of looking excited and happy for me, her face had turned a ghostly white. I thought she was going to faint. I had never seen her look so serious and scared before. Only two letters—HI—but it didn't appear to be a good sign from the look on my mom's face. I started to feel scared and out of control because I had no idea what was happening.

I sprinted to the bathroom and slammed the door shut in fear. Curling up in a ball, I screamed at the top of my lungs until I looked up and saw my three siblings standing in the doorway. Ever thoughtful as always, they were not going to let me go through this alone—whatever it was. My oldest sister has always been especially mothering, wanting to take care of all of her younger siblings. She reached down to hug me, and my other siblings joined in and assured me that whatever happened, it must have been a mistake.

After they had calmed me down, we went back into the kitchen, where I noticed that my mom was still standing in the doorway with that same blank stare she had had the night before. She picked up the phone, and we overheard her conversation with the doctor. The conversation was short and rushed, and the only words I could make out were "Okay, we will be right there."

She went into the living room and grabbed my dad. All she said to him was, "Brad, get in the car. Now." Without another word, she pushed me out the door and into the car. No one spoke a word during the entire car ride. The look on my mom's face told me her head was spinning so fast that she couldn't speak. I looked back to see my siblings staring out the window with worried faces as we drove off. Minutes later, I was in the emergency room of the local hospital. My mom's suspicions were right about the reason her glucometer simply read "HI" without any number. My blood sugar was so high that the meter couldn't even read it. The doctor's meter showed that I had a blood sugar level of 670, which is coma level, and I will never forget hearing the words, "I'm sorry, miss. She has juvenile diabetes," as they stabbed me with my first insulin shot. After receiving insulin that night, I immediately felt better, but I wasn't out of the woods yet. I had to go to a three-day training to learn how to check my blood sugar levels, give myself insulin shots, and change my diet to control my disease. It also helped explain my extreme thirst, the constant urge to pee, and the crazy mood swings I'd been experiencing, as all of those are symptoms of unchecked diabetes. Since my dad is also a type 1 diabetic, my mom knew that I would struggle with this for the rest of my life. Like my dad, I would never get a break from it, and it would drastically change my life in ways that I couldn't even imagine at the age of twelve.

I felt so bad that I had ruined Kaylee's sixteenth birthday, but I had to laugh later when I went home and heard my mom's cell phone ring and ring. Those were the days when everyone had a song for their ringtone, and since everyone was calling to check on me, her phone kept playing the same song over and over. It was that song "Bad Day" by Daniel Powter, and all I could think was how perfect it was for that moment, because we all had certainly had a very bad day indeed.

Crowning Achievement:

We were never promised to have no tribulations in life. We all have our own struggles. I know and have accepted that I will always have this disease. It was a journey to get through the anger and denial stages, but once I did, I learned to turn to God for help managing my feelings. He has helped me use my knowledge of health that I learned at a young age to help several people around the world with their health. Type 1 is not something humans bring on themselves, and it is not the type of diabetes that anyone can get rid of. I have taken four or more shots a day for fifteen years and check my blood sugar multiple times a day. And I'm okay with it. It has taught me that structure and discipline are important and that my differences may make my goals harder to achieve, but don't have to stop me. I have had hundreds of people reach out to me after seeing what I have accomplished in life with this disease, and they tell me that it gives them hope for their children who are living with type 1 diabetes. Whatever you may be going through, please never let your differences slow you down or stop you. Turn to God, as He will give you peace in all things.

Chapter 6

LOSING MIKE

If anyone has material possessions and sees a brother or sister in need but has no pity on them, how can the love of God be in that person? Dear Children, let us not love with words or speech but with action and truth.
1 John 3:17–18

Not long after my diabetes diagnosis, my mom had to go out of town for a conference, as she was working on her master's degree in education. After losing her daycare, she decided to become an elementary school teacher. With her away for the weekend, my dad, brother, and I went camping on my dad's farm with some of our extended family members. My sister Whitney was in college at this time, and Kaylee was in high school, so both were still living at home and could look after Mike so he wouldn't have to stay alone.

When I woke up the first morning and poked my head out of the tent, I saw my dad rush to his truck and speed away. I had no idea what was happening, but my aunt told me to come into the house so she could make me breakfast and I could check my blood sugar.

"What's going on?" I begged her. "Where did my dad go?"

She said, "Mackenzie, this isn't going to be easy to tell you, but you need to know. They found your brother not breathing this morning."

"Wait! What? *Who* found my brother dead?" I cried. She went on to break the news that my sisters had found Mike lifeless at home on the floor of the bathroom. They quickly called a nurse to come to perform CPR and get him in an ambulance.

The timing couldn't have been worse, with my mom out of town and us camping. My aunt told me to get dressed, and she rushed Zeke and me to the hospital. While waiting in the hallway, she kept stroking my hair and pulling me closer to her. I began to realize that if she was comforting me this much, it must be serious.

We had been waiting quite a while when my grandma rushed out yelling, "They found a heartbeat! They found a heartbeat!" The doctors had been able to revive Mike! But our relief and joy faded fast when we were told that even though he was breathing, he was brain-dead. Being so young, it was hard for me to process that once someone's brain is dead, he can't really come back to life. I thought that maybe he would make it. He would just sit up and start cracking jokes like he did when he broke his leg and got a cast a few months earlier. And even though his health had been going downhill since then, I knew Mike was a fighter and would be smiling again in no time. Seeing my sisters bawling in the corner of the hospital, though, led me to realize that even though he was technically alive, the Mike I knew and loved was gone.

My mom got the call about Mike and rushed home from the conference. No one was sure how much time he had left on life support. The nurses welcomed my mom into the ICU, and they let her stay with him. Later, she told us that in his final moments, she remembered talking to him and telling him how much she loved him. A tear fell down his face, and he passed. He was gone. It was almost like he wanted my mom to get there before he let go of life. He waited for his mama.

I had never experienced a loss like this in my life, so Mike's death was a real blow to me and my family. I learned so much from the blessing of having Mike in my life. He brought me to God more than anyone because, even though he had disabilities, he understood life, God, kindness, and humility much more than the average person. He taught me that what really matters in life isn't just working hard and making money. It was to have unconditional love for others. Sometimes to this day when things go wrong, I think about how so many of us are far away from the type of people we should be—loving, kind, and full of grace for others. Mike was all of these things.

Mike's funeral was huge, and it felt like everyone in Miami was there. People had to stand in the back of the church and its hallways because there weren't enough seats. It was a big church, and still it wouldn't hold all those people who came to pay their respects to the man who had melted so many hearts.

After the funeral service, Mike's aunt approached our family. From what we knew of her, she was an unhappy, stingy, and bitter old woman who tried to control every aspect of Mike's life. She was even the one who forced my mom to close her daycare because, she said, Mike didn't like having it at *his* home, which wasn't even true. She glanced quickly at all of us who were standing there crying and said, "I can't believe that this many people would come to a retarded man's funeral." That stung, and I was instantly ready to throw punches at her. *How dare she say something like that?* One of my sisters simply said, "She's an awful person, but she's the one who will have to live with who she is and what she said."

We really had no clue what Mike's life was like before he lived with us or what he heard others say about him, but we do know that his aunt didn't see him as a normal human being with wants and desires. When he wanted to marry and have children with a girl he loved named Becky, this same aunt quickly shut the idea down when my mom wanted to grant his wishes and plan a wedding. My mom always wanted to elevate Mike instead of keeping him down, and she even got him work at a furniture store so he could experience what it was like to have a job. When the owner of the store called her one day and told her that Mike was fired and to pick up her "retarded son," my mom stormed up there, let the owner have it, and walked out with Mike's hand in hers. Mike was fired for lowering prices on the furniture for families who couldn't afford it. He didn't realize he was breaking the rules, because he had such a sweet, gentle heart, but with my mom as his rock and protector, he felt at home by her side. He was a son, a brother, and a true and loyal friend, and I could tell that losing Mike was so hard for my mom. She was the one who opened up her heart and arms to a complete stranger and loved him dearly for eighteen years, and like always, she was a true example of letting God do his work by remaining kind to and accepting of everyone.

Mike played a crucial role in all of our lives, and he left an indelible mark on me. I'll never forget the time I came home from church camp and my mom had turned the dining room into my very own cowgirl-themed bedroom. I had wanted a room of my own so badly, but I never anticipated that the real gift I received wasn't the bedroom itself. The best surprise was that now I was only a wall away from Mike. He used to bug me sometimes by trying to talk to me through the walls at all hours of the night, but my friends loved staying the night and talking to him. I realized after he was gone how special it was to be so close and share those talks with Mike during those last years of his life.

I have heard that in some places it is legal for women to get an abortion if their baby has Down syndrome, and that's just heartbreaking to me, because I learned firsthand how people with disabilities have so much to offer the world. I will always have a place in my heart for people with special needs, and when I am around them, I feel like I can communicate with and connect to them. I don't stare or treat them as outcasts, and I have Mike to thank for that.

The night he passed was a very silent and lonely night, and I live on to say that whoever got to know him is a very lucky human. I miss you so much, Bub.

Crowning Achievement:

God made each and every one of us in his perfect image. He loved Mike and knew he had a purpose on Earth. Because my mom sees others the way God sees them, she is able to love everyone no matter who they are. We need to let go of material possessions, stereotypes, and thinking one human is better than the other. This world is such a beautiful place with different humans, races, and ways. Diversity is what makes all of God's creatures, great and small, so wonderful. Our job is to love everyone as Christ loves us.

Chapter 7

GIVING MYSELF AWAY

*Let no one despise you for your youth, but set the believers
an example in speech, in conduct, in love, in faith, in purity.*
1 Timothy 4:12

was a pretty angry human for those first few years of my diagnosis. After being diagnosed with type 1 diabetes and losing my brother Mike when I was fourteen years old, I desperately needed something positive to happen to me. As a result, I was ecstatic to finally get my first real boyfriend, and I hoped he could help turn my newly fractured world around. Many of my friends were diving headfirst into relationships, and I desperately wanted to fit in. They all looked like they were having so much fun coupling up, and I craved that kind of attention and wanted to feel special to someone other than my family. Feeling like I was always a disappointment to them, having a boy put all of his attention on me filled a void. Or so I thought.

I had had silly little middle school boyfriends but never anything serious. I dated one for months, and he broke up with me in a letter and humiliated me by telling the school I was too prudish. He was quickly shut up by my older brother, but not before word got back to me about what he had said. I hadn't even really kissed a boy, unless you count the little peck on the cheek that I gave my church boyfriend when we got "married" behind the shed of his parents' house when I was six. This was my first real crush, and I met him at a friend's house. He went to a school in the next town over. At the time, I thought he was so cute and popular, and he seemed to come along at just the right time. I had been suffering a lot. Learning to control my blood sugar, and the mood swings, brain fog, and anxiety that came along with that, was beyond exhausting. On top of that, losing my brother Mike had left a significant hole in my life. What better way to fill that hole with someone who would make me feel loved and accepted during this difficult time? That would surely help me forget my problems, right?

My incredible insecurities made me fall hard for this boy. I come from an amazingly wise and humble family; I truly believed they walked on water. We were such a close family, and I got to see the ins and outs and the good and the bad with them, although there didn't seem to be much bad. I sometimes wondered how I ended up with such an awesome family. I spent a lot of time looking in the mirror and wondering what was wrong with me. Why was I so different? Why do I struggle in school and have to take five insulin shots a day to control my diabetes? Why couldn't I have it easy and feel good once in a while? I thought I finally had it made. I was on cloud nine and felt so wanted.

My parents were not as thrilled with him as I was. They didn't feel that he was a good match for me, and it bothered my mom that he didn't follow Christ. I didn't let that stop me, though. This boy became my life. I spent time obsessing over him and trying to do everything to please him. After four months of dating, he convinced me that it was time we took things further intimately. He wasn't a virgin, but I was. I wanted to save myself for marriage, just like I had been taught was the right thing to do in God's eyes, but he explained that if I wasn't going to have sex with him, there were plenty of other girls out there who would. It would be easy for him to go out and find someone else. He also convinced me that this was normal and *everyone* else was doing it. I was never one to really party or do drugs, but for me, feeling accepted was a must, and this felt like one way I could fit in. I also couldn't forget in the back of my mind that I thought I'd already been "spoiled" from what those older boys did to me when I was a child. I mean, really, what did I have to lose? They had already stolen my innocence, hadn't they?

Due to the fear of losing him and the happiness I had finally felt at being in a relationship, I gave in. I won't go into detail, but I can assure you it was a miserable experience, and I remember thinking, *"I don't think this is how it's supposed to feel."* It hurt, and I begged him to stop, but he was doing his best to assure me that everything would be okay. Could I have said no and walked away? Yes. Did I? No. And I am aware that I chose to go along with his false facts that everyone does this and no boy will love me if I don't give in. He said I was the one who wasn't normal, which in my mind was one of the worst things someone could say because I wanted to fit in so badly. I believed him when he said that everyone I would date from here on out would want to have sex with me, so I figured I might as well go ahead and do it. I cried afterward and thought, *"Well, now he has to love and marry me."* That's how it is with sex, or so I had been taught. You had sex with someone, and they loved you. The next logical step was marriage, according to what I had learned at church, and I was only going to have sex with my husband like God wanted. I also knew that my parents had only been with each other, and they got pregnant before marriage, and love and marriage came next for them. So I thought that must be how things work out for everyone, right?

The next day I felt awful. I couldn't believe that I had caved to his demands, and now I had to find a way to live with what I did. I remember the feeling of going home, lying in my bed, and feeling guilty, nervous, and less loved than I had before. I knew in my heart that this couldn't be the way I was supposed to feel or what God wanted for me. Maybe if I kept it a secret, it would feel like it didn't really happen.

I continued to date this boy, and I kept doing everything I could to make him happy and prevent him from leaving me, even though he was controlling. I craved his approval, and I worked hard to have the perfect hair, makeup, and body to please him. We dated for almost two years—two long, miserable, controlling years. We were young and dumb. Both of us, honestly.

On Valentine's Day during the second year we were dating, he told me to get dressed up, because he was going to take me on a special date. I was so excited, and I tried to look as pretty as I could for him. I curled my hair, did my makeup, and put on a dress that I knew he liked on me. I was ready at 6:00 PM, the time he said he would pick me up. Well, 6:00 PM came and went. I didn't have a cell phone, so I tried calling him on my parents' home phone. I called and called, but I got no answer. Midnight passed. Still nothing, and no phone calls. I stayed dressed up until 3:00 AM, and he never came. How dumb and desperate could I be? I was completely devastated and cried my eyes out. I was sure my life was over. Oh, the things I wish I could go back and tell myself in that moment! I didn't want to talk to my mom about it because she had warned me about boys who only want "one thing" from you, and she was right. I did not want to hear, "I told you so." The next day, I went to school depressed and running on no sleep. My eyes were still puffy from all the crying. I remember sitting in class when someone behind me tapped my shoulder. It was one of my older brother Zeke's friends. Zeke was a strong, well-respected football player only a grade older than I, and although his friends would never date me due to being scared of him, they always had my back and saw me as a little sister. This boy said he *needed* to tell me something important. He told me he had seen my boyfriend the night before at a party making out with another girl. Not only that, but he went on to spill the details that my boyfriend had slept with several other girls—many of them were my own friends—the *whole two years* that he and I had been dating. With how much he tried to control me, this was shocking, but now I know a key red flag for men who are controlling. Now I knew why my parents did not want me to be with this kid, and I was nowhere near prepared for the heartbreak about to hit me.

"That's it," I thought. "This is over." I have never been one to let someone hurt me and not give them back the revenge I thought they deserved, and I was pretty desperate to get this pain off my mind. My friend invited me to a school basketball game, and I eagerly accepted the invite. I was ready to get out and get my mind off of things. She had some friends she wanted to see.

When we got to the game, I saw a good family friend from church in the crowd. I waved at him and caught his eye, and he yelled, "Big Mac! Come over here!" Running up to where he was sitting, I immediately gave him a huge hug. Sensing another pair of eyes on me as we hugged, I turned to see he had another friend with him—one I'd never met. "Hey, I want to introduce you to my friend," he said.

The boy whom he introduced me to was so shy that I practically had to force him to give me a handshake. He was wearing cowboy boots, jeans, and a cutoff shirt, and I was instantly drawn to him. He was tall, dark, and handsome. He was chewing tobacco, and honestly, he was so redneck looking, but it didn't faze me because a lot of guys in my little hometown looked similar. He didn't say anything else, but he kept smiling and looking over at my friend and me. Wanting to see if any of our other friends were there, we said goodbyes for the moment and took off.

When the game was over, my friend and I hopped into her truck to go home. We were still giggling about that cute but awkward boy. My friend admitted that she thought he was awfully attractive. "I think he kind of liked me," she said excitedly. "Did you see how he kept looking over and smiling at us?"

Even though I obviously thought he was pretty cute, too, I would never break girl code. Ever. If one of my friends liked or dated a man, he would be off-limits to me for the rest of my life. I've made more than my share of mistakes, but being loyal to my girls is something I've never messed up. After she showed interest in him, I let it go and forgot about liking him.

To be honest, I also knew that now was not the best time to start chasing other guys. I had only just broken up with my ex for cheating on me, and I hadn't really had time to process the whole mess. It was going to take a long time to build back the self-respect I had lost when I caved in to his desires. Had I loved myself more, I would have said no and realized that this boy didn't *truly* love me. I regretted that someday when I did get married, I wouldn't be able to tell my husband that I had never been intimate with anyone else but him. Getting over this breakup might finally give me the confidence and self-esteem to hold my head high with my crown straight and not give in to the demands of any man.

As I was getting out of the truck when she dropped me off back at home, my friend stopped one more time to ask another question. "Hey! Do you remember what his name was?"

"Yes," I answered. "His name was Josh. Josh McKee."

Crowning Achievement:

If I could go back and change anything in life, I would love and respect myself more. I was young, but I was not living in purity. This is something I'm prepared to talk to my children about. I want my boys to respect girls and my daughter to know that any man who truly loves you will wait to have sex before marriage. Sex is meant to unite two people physically, emotionally, and spiritually, and giving yourself to someone who doesn't love you only destroys you deep inside.

Chapter 8

JUST GO FOR IT

*So in everything, do to others what you would have them
do to you. For this sums up the law and the prophets.*
Matthew 7:12

had been hanging out with the wrong crowd as a freshman in
high school. My brother Mike had passed away, I was diagnosed with a scary illness, and I broke up with my first boyfriend. I knew I needed to pick myself up, dust myself off, and
stand up straight again, but I wasn't sure how. And then Josh
came along.

Remember how I said I never break girl code? Well, even
though I thought Josh was cute, my friend saw him first. Before
I could even search, I saw that I had a MySpace message. It was
from him. It said: "Hi, Mackenzie. I thought you were so pretty

when we met tonight. Would you like to go out with me some-time?" My heart raced as I felt adrenaline rush through my body. But then I remembered my friend. My heart sank.

Wanting to be completely transparent, I showed my friend his message the next day. "Oh, that message is so sweet, and he's so cute! You have to go out with him," she said. Still hesitant, I said, "But you liked him first. Girl code, you know?"

"Whatever!" she said. "Just go for it! You have to!" That's when I messaged him back.

Being so young, just fifteen, I didn't even yet have my driver's license. That's how young we were—we were still just kids! He made his friend drive him on our first date, which was to see the movie *Valentine*. It's ironic how I had such a horrible Valentine's Day waiting for the boyfriend who never showed up, and here I was just ten days later on a date with Josh. I was determined that this "Valentine" would turn out better than the last.

I really don't remember a darn thing about that movie because we talked all the way through it. What drew me to Josh was his calm and even manner. As someone who is hyper and wants to do all the talking, I loved this quality in him. He had the ability to put me at ease as he told me about his life and his passions. He oozed Southern charm, not even putting his arm around me or holding my hand during the movie. I actually wanted him to grab me and kiss me right there in the theater, but nope. At first, I thought maybe he was just nervous, but I quickly learned that was just Josh. What a change from my last boyfriend! My ex was hyper and energetic like me, and that drove me nuts! Balance in relationships matters. I never wanted to be with someone like that again, because that's too much like me. Josh, on the other hand, was so laid-back and calm. And to top it off, he said he loved God. Since I didn't even have to bring that up first, that was very attractive to me, as my last boyfriend didn't believe in God at all. We didn't have that connection where we could talk about God together, so this made me start falling for Josh even harder.

After that first date, things got serious. I mean, Josh wanted to marry me within a month! He was head over heels, and so was I. He was all I talked about and thought about, and we started spending most of our free time together. School would get out, and I'd go to his house. He lived in the country, and he loved riding horses and being outside—exactly my type of guy. As a homebody and an introvert, Josh wanted to stay home and be in nature instead of going to wild parties or hanging out with big groups of friends. He wanted to do things where we could be alone and he could have me all to himself, so we would go coyote hunting, fish, ride horses, walk dogs, you name it. The two of us had so much in common. We were both the babies of our families, and we both were enamored with animals. Josh was good with animals, and like me, he dreamed of owning all kinds someday on a farm of his own.

One time, we were driving down some country roads in his truck when we spotted a sign that read "Chickens for sale." "Oh, please, Josh! Can we stop and get some? Please, please!" I begged. He pulled the truck over and bought me ten chickens right then and there. We took them to his house on the farm, and I would come over every day after school to come and love on my chickens. That's the kind of guy Josh was—not one who would bring flowers and candy, but one who would buy chickens for me on the spot. I couldn't have wanted him any other way.

Since we were so in love and inseparable, I took him home to meet my parents. Unlike my last boyfriend, they loved Josh from day one. The fact that Josh and I met in Wyandotte, Oklahoma—the same place my parents met—seemed like fate. It was smooth sailing, and we were meant to be.

The only place where Josh and I seemed to differ is that he was a homebody and would prefer to stay in rather than go out and party with friends. I wanted to be with other people and have fun. I was on the cheer squad and loved hanging out, so I would just have to go out with my friends behind his back and then have my separate time with Josh. I felt bad about doing that, but it was the only thing that bothered me at the time about our relationship. Since I wasn't doing anything bad while he stayed at home, I figured no one would get hurt.

Shortly after that first date, my ex started trying to creep back into my life by calling me and asking if I was dating Josh. I told him yes, and that we've kissed and dated. I guess I had chased this ex-boyfriend for so long, that when I finally moved on, he got jealous and wanted me back. After all, he and Josh went to the same school and hung out in the same crowd. They were buddies. He explained that there were only thirty people in their graduating class, and everyone knew how much people in small towns liked to gossip. But I have to admit, telling him about kissing and dating Josh gave me a feeling of satisfaction. I had never been able to stand up to him and talk to him like that.

I still knew a relationship with this guy wasn't going to last long term. His family didn't like me, and my family was not exactly fond of him. But he kept calling and telling me he wanted me back. Instead of learning my lesson the first time that God had broken us up to save me from forever walking on eggshells to please this guy—the one who had cheated on me with all my friends—I ended up going over to his house. I didn't know what to do with the emotions I was feeling. This guy who I thought I had loved and who I lost my virginity to finally wanted me as much as I had once wanted him. He was telling me how much he missed me and needed to see me. Still dealing with lingering feelings about him, I thought that maybe seeing him one last time would reaffirm my feelings for Josh, but what started out as seeing my ex just one last time turned out to be more.

I'm not proud to admit this part of my life. I made the same mistake with him more than once. Many people wonder how I could have done this if Josh and I were so in love. While I can't excuse what I did, I was so young and didn't know what to do with the emotions I was still feeling for my ex. I wouldn't exactly call it love, but more so being young and dumb.

Of course, Josh eventually found out I was cheating, and I felt guilt sinking in. I was sick to my stomach for going behind his back and hurting him. A little bit of fun on the side with my ex was not worth the heartache and pain that I caused Josh. It also didn't boost my self-worth to know that my ex was still attracted to me and wanted me back. He didn't love me. I did all this for a guy who cheated on me with my friends and crushed my self-esteem. He had broken me, and I foolishly went back for more, not realizing how much damage this could do to Josh and our budding relationship.

If I could take anything back about that time, I would never have been unfaithful to Josh. I think it was just so early on in our relationship, and I figured that if my ex could hurt me so badly, Josh would likely be next. But in cheating, I set the standard of unfaithfulness in our relationship. I had no idea how hard it would be to turn things around after cheating. It was difficult for me to understand then and now how I could do those things when what I really wanted was a life with Josh.

When Josh found out, he suddenly just stopped talking to me. Our relationship seemed to be hanging in the balance until I found out from a friend that Josh had messed around with another girl at a party. He claimed that we weren't together anymore, so he wasn't cheating, but we had never officially broken up. I was so hurt, and this just added more fuel to the fire, but I figured if that was the way he saw it, then I could continue to sleep with my ex since any time I wanted *him* to be there, he would. I was broken, but I wouldn't get back with him. I would use him this time instead of letting him use me.

Josh and I separated for a while, but somehow, we just kept gravitating back toward one another. Josh knew all about my ex and me, and he had the patience of a saint. He didn't want to talk about it, but he had forgiveness in his heart. I vowed never to cheat again, and he did the same. Gradually, things started falling back in place, and we felt we were madly in love again.

Even though Josh and I had started sleeping together relatively early on in our relationship, I felt things were different this time. With Josh, I knew we were in love and that he was the one I wanted to be with forever. He felt the same way. After working out those early ups and downs, we talked about getting married, even though we were so young. We were confident that we were each other's "person" and that we could make things work. How could anything go wrong now? We were crazy about each other.

No matter how wild I got when we were apart, I always wanted a perfect life with Josh. I wanted my perfect family. I just didn't realize it was all about to happen so soon.

Crowning Achievement:

We all know the Golden Rule: Do unto others as you would want done unto you. This comes from the book of Matthew in the Bible, and it's a rule that never loses its value. If every human treated others as they want to be treated, the world would be a much better place. No one would have ever been beaten, cheated on, murdered, robbed, or treated unequally. But, because we are human and sinners, we stray away from following this rule. If I could go back and change things, I would treat Josh how I'd want him to treat me at the beginning of our relationship. I was hurt by my first real boyfriend, so I hardened my heart, and I allowed myself to hurt others. The Golden Rule is so simple and helps us to be strong and not let those who hurt us dictate who we are deep inside.

Chapter 9

LATE

For you created my inmost being, you knit me together in my mother's womb. I praise you because I am fearfully and wonderfully made. Your works are wonderful, I know that full well.
Psalm 139:13–14

"Josh, I'm late. I missed my period."
These are words that most sixteen-year-old girls never want to utter, and most sixteen-year-old boys never want to hear. But I had a hunch. A big hunch. My body just didn't feel right. My sugars were high, and I was so fatigued all the time now. I tried to power through it and pretend that this may not be a possibility, but I vividly remember being at cross-country practice and barely making it through the miles. A thought crossed my mind—*what if I'm pregnant?* It was certainly possible, but I knew

Josh and I weren't ready to be parents. Still, I had to be sure. I started thinking about how I could get a pregnancy test without anyone finding out.

I snuck out to the local drugstore with my heart racing. What if someone saw me? What if they told my parents? I didn't even know what to buy! At the back of the store, I found the pregnancy tests, but I was so nervous to buy one that I considered stealing it. Not only was I sneaking around to buy the test, but if I were to steal it and get caught, the whole town would be talking about me! Looking around to make sure no one saw me, I grabbed two tests. One wouldn't do the trick. I needed two tests to be completely certain.

I went up to the counter and dug around in my purse for some money. I scraped up enough change and dollar bills, and I put the tests on the checkout counter. What I wouldn't have given for self-checkout at that time, but, sadly, those didn't exist yet. I was so little and skinny—not even five feet tall—that I still looked like a child, and I'm sure the woman at the counter wondered why in the world a little kid was buying pregnancy tests. I slapped the money down on the counter and ran out before anyone else could notice me. I hurried to Josh's house where we could finally stop wondering and, hopefully, stop worrying.

When I got there, Josh whisked me in through the door and into the bathroom. I took the test in front of him, and we waited for what seemed like an hour. Only a few minutes later, we looked down and saw the results. Positive. Pregnant.

Josh didn't believe the test was accurate and said, "Those things don't work. Give me one of those. I'll take it! I'll bet you it will say I'm pregnant." He snatched the unused test out of my hand and peed on the stick. Of course, it was negative, and we both realized we were in for a long night.

We talked and talked, and Josh seemed excited—maybe even more excited than I was—at the thought of welcoming a baby. I was conflicted, however. I loved Josh and wanted to marry him and have a child with him, but what about becoming a college cheerleader? Would I ever get to be a cheer coach as I'd planned? Now it seemed that my whole life was up in the air.

My mom made my first doctor's appointment shortly after she came around to the idea of helping me raise my baby. And, just as she drove me all around to gymnastics, she vowed to take me to every doctor's appointment.

I was nervous seeing the doctor that first time because I really had no idea what to expect. The doctor was female, which I was hoping would take away some of my fears. When she walked into the exam room, the doctor looked straight at my mom and said, "First, I'd like to ask you why you let your sixteen-year-old daughter get pregnant."

I will never forget the way my mom responded. She said, "That's not why we're here. We're here for medical attention. That's your job, so give us the answers we need."

The doctor went on to say that if I had this baby, there was a 30 percent chance I would die and an 80 percent chance of the baby dying—if not both of us. That's how bad my diabetes had gotten. I'd been so angry that I had the disease that I felt the best way to deal with it was just to ignore it. I hadn't been taking my insulin shots or eating the way I should, and as a result, I was weak, and my eyesight was getting ruined. I was going to die if I didn't start taking diabetes seriously, but nothing had gotten through to me thus far. Now, I was finding out the hard truth.

There was a serious chance that due to the careless way I was taking care of myself, both my baby and I could die.

The doctor continued trying to convince my mom why having this baby was a terrible idea. She explained that my A1C (which is a three-month average of your blood sugar readings) was dangerously high. So, she kept repeating to my mom that the baby wasn't going to live. "If you love your daughter, you will go get her an abortion. She is way too young, she is a diabetic, and she's high-risk. For her safety, if you care about her, she needs to go get an abortion now."

I already knew how my mom felt about abortions because she had told me once about a friend who had one. As teenagers, they were pregnant with their first babies at the same time. While my mom chose to keep her baby, the other woman decided to get an abortion. My mom didn't judge her and continued to love her. That's what she chose and felt was the right decision for her. But my mom remembered meeting up with her five years later, and the friend said that she had been on depression medication since the abortion, and it was hard for her to look at my mom's baby. They were still friends, but my mom said she was never the same, and my mom didn't want that kind of sadness for me.

I have several friends who have had abortions, but I can honestly say the thought never crossed my mind to get one. It's everyone's individual choice, and I don't think someone is a horrible person if they make that choice. I am no saint, so I choose to not judge, but I just knew I couldn't do it. We can't pretend to know what a particular situation feels like unless we've experienced it ourselves. In my situation, I knew that getting an abortion would leave me with guilt and sorrow; however, I believe getting an abortion is not something that separates a woman from the Lord. Nor is it the unforgivable sin that some Christians say it is.

Every one of us is more alike than we know. We all have our own issues, and no one individual is better than the other.

At that moment, my mom turned to the doctor and said, "That's not why we're here. She's going to have this baby." And with that, she grabbed my arm, and we marched out of the office. We never went back to that doctor again.

Crowning Achievement:

The book of Psalms explains how unique we are. God loves us so much that he knit us together exactly how he wanted us. As sinful humans, we chose to decide on our own what "good" looks like, but everyone matters to God. Sometimes, I wonder if I'm not good enough, but this verse also teaches us that every human on this Earth is good enough in God's eyes—just like I knew from the second I saw that positive test that my unborn baby mattered. That is why it's important to turn to Him instead of only seeking to gain acceptance from other humans.

Chapter 10

16 & PREGNANT

Humble yourselves before the Lord, and he will lift you up.
James 4:10

While my new doctor went above and beyond to make sure I was happy and healthy during pregnancy, people in my town had different thoughts. Word had gotten around that I was pregnant, and some rumors were spreading that the baby might not be Josh's. That's definitely some typical small-town talk for you, but there was no possible way that the baby belonged to my ex. Zero chance. I know it was extremely tough for Josh to have people whisper about us behind our backs.

I wish I could say that's where the gossip ended, but that was hardly the case. Even though a lot of my friends were out partying, drinking, and sleeping with different men, their parents didn't want me to be around their kids because I was the "bad one" who got pregnant.

Another rumor that got back to me was that one of my cheer coaches didn't want me on the squad because I was a "bad example." She was afraid that students and parents would be too embarrassed to be known as the school with the teen mom on the squad. I had heard these same people say hurtful things about other girls who had had abortions, and here I was making the difficult choice to have my baby only to be shunned for getting pregnant in the first place. I tried hard to shake off the rude and hurtful things I heard about myself. Before all this happened to me, I was probably a pretty judgmental person, too, but going through this started to really change and humble me. I was certain that I had made the right decision to have this baby, but it was hard with so many people looking down on me.

One thing that helped ease the pain was that we found out we were having a boy! I was so excited to have a little boy. I was always scared to have a girl because of the traumatic things I had gone through myself as a kid, and I was so hard to raise. I was absolutely sure that she would carry my genes and be a handful. I wanted a little country boy with Josh's laid-back demeanor. I wondered excitedly what he would look like, since I have blonde hair and blue eyes, and Josh has dark handsome Native features.

Determined to have a healthy and safe pregnancy, I decided that I needed to turn things around and start looking out for my well-being. I started checking my blood sugar and taking my insulin shots on schedule, and I went on a strict diabetic diet. Never before had I been so on top of things! I was already calling this baby a miracle and my saving grace, because he was the only one who could convince me to start paying attention to my health. He wasn't even born yet, but he was saving my life.

While looking for tips on managing my diabetes, I found a group on Facebook for diabetic moms. I joined and wrote my first post to the group, telling them that I was diabetic and pregnant, and I was only sixteen. There had to be someone with similar experiences to share with me. Not long after that first post, someone replied. "Hey, have you seen that MTV show *16 & Pregnant*? You have an interesting story—you should be on that show!"

I had heard of *16 & Pregnant,* but I had never seen it because my parents didn't allow me to watch MTV. Still, I was intrigued by the thought of being on TV. I called my sister Kaylee into my room and asked her to read this woman's response. Kaylee said, "Let's see if they're casting," and we went on the MTV website.

As luck would have it, MTV happened to be casting the show at that very time, so we laughed as Kaylee wrote a quick email and hit "send" before I could stop her. I honestly never expected to hear anything back. In fact, I had pretty much forgotten all about it until one afternoon at school about a month later.

All athletes at my school were required to take mandatory drug tests to be eligible to play in that week's games, and the cheer squad was no exception. My friends and I were in the restroom taking our tests, and I literally got a call in the bathroom stall while I was peeing into a cup. I almost thought it was a joke at first, but it started to sink in the more I heard. It was someone from MTV who explained that a film crew wanted to come to Oklahoma next week to interview me and do a test run to see if I would be right for the show. They would follow me around for a few days and film my actions. If they liked the way the footage went and they felt I was right for the show, that would be it—I'd be a part of the cast! I couldn't believe it. After a brief pause, I said, "Let me ask my mom if that's okay. I'll call you back," and I hung up the phone. It seems funny to think that although I was about to *be* a parent, I still had to *ask my own parents* for permission! It's also pretty funny to think that one of the most influential moments in my life occurred in a restroom stall at my high school. It seemed so unreal at the time.

The next period in algebra, my hands were shaking from excitement. I texted my mom to tell her that some people from MTV in New York wanted to talk to me about being on a show called *16 & Pregnant.* I tried to explain that this wasn't a done deal and give the impression that I probably wouldn't get chosen anyway. She had no idea that they were basically going to be filming my segments for what would be my whole first episode! It still makes me laugh to think that here I was—a teenager in math class whose mom wouldn't even let her *watch* MTV, and now she was asking her mom's permission to be *on* MTV. Surprisingly, my mom showed interest right away, and she had already thought of an important question she wanted to ask the show's producer: *If our family was going to be on TV, would they let my mom talk about her love for God?* With still no idea if my film footage would actually even air on TV, I promised to ask on her behalf, and I already knew this could go a long way toward getting my mom to agree.

My mom knew our small church probably wouldn't like the idea of us being on MTV and the picture it might paint of our church, but she knew that God wouldn't care as long as she could spread His word. She could be on MTV and tell viewers that they needed Christ in their lives. "I don't need to be on a Christian TV channel where all the Christians already are," she said. "But on MTV, I could possibly reach many nonbelievers or people who may have turned away from God. I can help more people find their way to Christ who might not otherwise have the chance to be saved." Trust me when I say that she had several adults tell her how risky this was.

The only person I didn't tell, though, was Josh. I thought I should keep it a secret from him for the time being, because I already knew he wouldn't like this idea at all. I kept trying to think of a way to break the news to him, but since I'd already told a few friends, word would be getting around my school in no time at all. I knew he was going to find out from someone else if I didn't tell him soon, and I'd rather he heard it from me than through small-town gossip. I was worried that he wouldn't be thrilled, though. He's not the type who likes a spotlight shining on him, and he doesn't exactly have what anyone would probably call a "TV personality," since he's so quiet and reserved.

That same afternoon that MTV called, my mom took me to a doctor's appointment, and we heard the baby's heartbeat for the first time. I felt a rush of happiness and excitement that I'd never experienced before. Leaving the office, I realized it was time to tell Josh about the show, but I wanted to see what he would say about it *before* I told him the film crew was actually on their way to Oklahoma to film us. I had my mom drop me off at his house and kept things simple by asking, "How would you feel about us being on TV?" I eagerly awaited his response.

"Oh, *hell no*," he quickly responded. "I'm *not* going to be on any TV show." That was all he had to say—equally short and straight to the point.

If you know me, you know I refuse to be controlled. It's something I'm still working on to this day. I let my first boyfriend control me, and once I broke up with him, I promised myself I would live freely from then on. I told him flat-out that I was going to do the show with or without him. It was obvious to me that he didn't want to do this, as I watched him pace back and forth in his room, shaking his head. He understood that I was going to do it regardless of his opinions, and since he didn't want to lose me, he reluctantly agreed to do the show too. In retrospect, I'm pretty sure that neither of us knew what we were getting ourselves into and how quickly the world as we knew it would change.

It's a good thing I told Josh when I did because word of the show started spreading around the town like wildfire. People were buzzing about the chance to see Miami, Oklahoma, on TV and maybe get their few minutes of fame. On the other hand, some people were clearly not happy about Miami's upcoming moment in the spotlight, and I had to withstand a lot of dirty looks when I was out.

I had a part-time job at a daycare center, and it was obvious the owners had heard about the show, because they called me in their office one afternoon shortly after it was announced that I was being considered for the show, and the owners screamed at me. They said that this was a church daycare and that the film crew wouldn't be allowed to film anything on-site or step foot inside, because, according to them, moms were going to get embarrassed and start pulling their kids out. They went on a big rant about losing money and how immoral this would be for me to go through with. I went home from work that night confused at how angry the daycare owners were. When I went to work the next day, they called me into the office again. What could be wrong now? All they said was that this was my last day on the job. I would have to leave immediately and take all of my things home with me. I was fired. They gave me no reason at all, and I couldn't imagine what I had done to deserve this.

I went home bawling. Not only was I pregnant, but I was also poor. How would I be able to support this baby now without a job? When I got home, my mom saw me crying and said, "Mackenzie, surely you did something." I told her I had done nothing worthy of getting fired, but that some of the other workers had told the owners that I was going to be on a TV show about being a teen mom, and they thought it was going to ruin their business and their reputation. This show was already causing people to hate me, and nothing had even come about yet.

My mom wasn't having it. She immediately picked up the phone and called to ask them why I was fired since they hadn't given me a reason. They told her that they had seen me eat a baby puff while feeding the babies the day before. "It's protocol that we don't do that," they told her.

Yep, that's right. I got fired for doing something I saw the other girls do every day. I had stuck a baby puff in my mouth and eaten it, and they said that is why they fired me.

My mom, still upset, asked, "Is that really why she was fired, or is this because of the show?" I don't remember how that conversation ended, but I remember that after she hung up the phone, she was very disappointed.

The church that both my mom and I were raised in decided not to allow cameras when we went to church, which was disappointing because it was such a huge part of our story; however, we always respected peoples' wishes when it came to MTV. We just didn't expect it to go how it did. The church meant a lot to us, and because the minister's family was good friends with my family (and still is to this day), it was a tough decision for him to make. But preachers have to make decisions in the best interest of their churches, so I understood his point of view.

Out of all the painful things that happened, the thing that stung the most was when a mom pulled her kids from the youth group because I, a pregnant teen, was in there. I thought that the Christian thing to do was to love and accept everyone while letting God be the judge of all. I have to admit that this started pulling me even further away from God. "Okay, God, so I can't even go to church now or be in the youth group? I made a mistake, and I'm getting banished?"

While some church members were saying negative things about my mom and me, a big portion of the congregation did show plenty of support. As a matter of fact, most of my nurses were from the church. I was terrified that my mom would blame me for ruining her reputation, as well as her relationship with the church and God, but she never did. My mom stood up for me. She had already had her poster-ripping moment of anger with me. She was over it.

My family continued to go to church. I remained in the youth group, even though a few people pulled their kids out because of me. Even when many of the church elders stopped talking to me, my mom never got embarrassed. She said that we weren't going to be embarrassed and that we would walk into church, hold our heads up high, and she would be holding my hand the entire time. My mom was so into her faith in God, and she handled it so differently than people thought she would. She wasn't going to hate people, especially her own children, because they made mistakes. She had so much grace and forgiveness, and I will tell you, it did not pass down to me. I was angry and resentful at the way people were treating me. It just wasn't right.

My mom's dedication didn't stop there, either. She went with me to all of my doctor's appointments and remained by my side when it seemed no one else would. I had acted terribly toward my mom and had been so mean to her as I was growing up. Why did she always stick by me and give me so many chances? My mom gave me so much, but the most valuable things she imparted to me were her wisdom and grace when facing hardships. She never let it get her (or me) down, and I try to have her strength every day when life gets rough.

My siblings also heard what people were saying about me behind my back, but they protected me from the gossip so I wouldn't get hurt. My mom's love and grace really shined through them at this time. They never expected the *baby* of the family to be *having* a baby first. Although they were disappointed in my life choices, they were always there with a shoulder I could lean on. Zeke, just one grade above me, rode the school bus with me and sat by my side. He was strong and respected by his peers, and he always checked on me to make sure no one picked on me. We were so close that one day a teenage girl came up to us on the bus and said that our baby was going to be beautiful! We looked at each other and laughed uncontrollably, explaining to her that he was my brother and was just looking out for me.

Crowning Achievement:

Just as the book of James states, my siblings humbled themselves during a difficult time, and this helped me become more humble, as I felt I had an entire town judging me. It was a challenge that no one in my family asked for, but we all stayed fixed on God, and He truly carried us all. It made us an easy target of gossip, and I can't say that I would not have been judgmental if someone else had gotten pregnant in a Christian family in my town and ended up on TV. The fact that I went through this, though, taught me to be less judgmental of others and love them for who they are—not who we think they should be.

Chapter 11

"MOM, MTV IS HERE!"

But godliness with contentment is great gain. For we brought nothing into the world, and we can take nothing out of it. But if we have food and clothing, we will be content with that.
1 Timothy 6:6–12

Those few weeks before the film crew arrived just flew by, and the next thing I knew, their vans were parked outside our home. They came out and fell in love with my family and how our story was so different. We were such a strong, close-knit family with solid faith in each other and God. My mom was truly in her element as she welcomed them all into our home. It must have been more than a little scary for some of the diverse crew to land in nondiverse Miami, Oklahoma, but my mom opened her arms to them all. The crew also found my dad quite entertaining. The first time they met him and went to shake his hand, my dad happened to be cleaning fish guts so we could have a fish fry that night, and he was wearing a T-shirt that said "Pull My Finger" with a fart emoji. They knew that they were in for a fun time with us.

It all started out so positive and simple. They said that they'd be following me around for the week, filming my interactions with friends, the cheer squad, my family, and Josh. When they said they'd follow me, I imagined one van would shadow me wherever I went, but in reality, four vans covered my every step. We were hard to miss.

One of the first scenes that they filmed for the show was of my friends and I going to a rodeo to watch Josh. We found a place to sit in the stands, and people stared at us while the camera watched our every move. Of course, I was excited for the chance to be on TV—who wouldn't be? My friends were good sports and allowed themselves to be filmed, even though their parents had to sign off for them since we were all underage. We had a great time at the rodeo, pretending that we didn't have several cameras in our faces. But, as we sat there, I couldn't help but catch the dirty looks coming from the bleachers surrounding us. There was some serious side-eye going on, and it was no secret that the people of my hometown were sickened to see these city slickers descending on our little town and giving me attention for being a pregnant teen.

Josh didn't seem to have a lot of sympathy when I told him about it after the rodeo. "What did you expect, Mackenzie? People don't want that here. They don't want to be in the spotlight, and they don't understand why you do. They just want to live their lives in peace without worrying they'll end up on TV." He didn't hold back at all, and I could tell he felt the same way.

I felt bad, but at the same time, wasn't this also my choice? I was the one who was sixteen and pregnant—the one with the story to tell. I wanted to tell my story, and if fame came along with it, I wasn't going to complain.

If I still had any doubt about how my community felt about the show and me, it was gone the next morning when I walked outside. Someone had scrawled "Attention Whore" across the windshield of my car, along with a photo of dripping boobs that said, "Got milk?" Once again, I felt that familiar sense of humiliation creep through my body. Why couldn't I live the life I wanted and everyone else just leave me alone?

Not long after the TV cameras had stopped rolling and the filming crew left Miami, Josh planned a special date for us. I think he was just really happy to have the show behind us so we could go back to our normal, everyday lives. That day, we went to a park with a beautiful view of a lake. As we were walking around, Josh got down on one knee and proposed. He said he loved me and wanted to spend the rest of his life with me, then he gave me a ring that his mom had taken him to the store to pick out. While I loved Josh and wanted to marry him, I was more than a little disappointed in his proposal. Instead of planning something big and extravagant that I would like, he chose to ask me in this quiet and secluded park. Looking back now, I can see that Josh was trying to be romantic and sweet, but at that time of my life, I wanted something the whole world could see. Despite my disappointment in the proposal, I said yes. I loved him and was pregnant with his child, so I wanted to give this a chance. I just wish I would have enjoyed that moment more. It has taken me some time and growing up to savor these kinds of moments, because it's not all about what the rest of the world sees and thinks.

Getting engaged did not stop our fighting, however. We would get into fights, and I would throw my ring at him. Then, the next day, I'd put it back on. I would take it off again when I went to a party and then put it back on when I'd see Josh. I was honestly not a great girlfriend at the time, and with all the fighting that we'd been doing lately, Josh hadn't always been the best boyfriend, either. We were going to have to figure things out soon, though, because it wouldn't be long now until we'd be adding another little heart to this family.

Crowning Achievement:

I fell into the sinful nature of materialism, and this made me a true brat. If it wasn't top of the line or the way I had pictured it in my head, I wasn't happy. Once I learned to be content, my relationship with God grew, and I became a better person within.

Chapter 12

WELCOMING GANNON

Before I formed you in the womb, I knew you.
Before you were born I set you apart.
Jeremiah 1:5

That summer of pregnancy was a blast. My *16 & Pregnant* producer stayed in town for an entire month until I had the baby. She would bring me treats and just sit and talk with me. I loved it, because when everyone was at work and school, I was on bed rest and could hang out with her as a friend. I had a few other great friends who were happy just going to the creek with me instead of a crazy party, and we became so close that we're still friends today. If I wasn't with them, I was right by my mom's side—way more than I was at Josh's. He hated the cameras and that my entire pregnancy was being documented.

My mom and I did everything that summer. We would shop for the baby, swim, go on long walks, and sit in her backyard and laugh. Since I couldn't exactly sneak out and go party with friends, my mom and I became super close. My whole family would talk about how perfect this baby would be, and we finally began to put all the small-town talk aside and get excited.

As my due date approached, my doctor told me that the baby already weighed close to ten pounds, and I still had a month to go! It wasn't really a surprise, as type 1 and gestational diabetics tend to have large babies. What *was* a surprise, however, was the night the baby decided to arrive.

I was with my family at my brother's football game, and it felt like all eyes were staring at my giant belly. During the game, I told my mom that I was experiencing sharp pains, and they were getting worse. At 3:00 AM that night, we called my producer, and she rushed over to film my mom and me as we headed to the hospital. Josh had been up all night worrying about me, so my mom called him and told him to get to the hospital too. We couldn't believe it was time to have the baby!

Once we got to the hospital, the doctor decided it was time for me to have a C-section, but he needed to check the baby's lungs first. As an overdramatic teen, try as I might, it was hard to stay calm. The doctor stuck a giant needle right in the center of my stomach, and as we looked at the ultrasound, I heard my mom say, "Oh, no." The baby's little hand was punching on the needle! My mom knew it was time to squeeze my hand at that moment, and I let out a loud scream.

We were barely through that experience when I was rolled back to the surgery room, where I had to endure another huge needle. All of the nurses were longtime church friends who held me and prayed fiercely while an epidural needle pierced my spine.

While this was going on, my family piled up in the waiting room and played a guessing game of the baby's weight.

With a bright light in my face and nurses running around prepping me for surgery, I was feeling very emotional. I was only allowed to bring one person into the delivery room, but since they knew us, they let both my mom and Josh stay. I remember they both had their hands on my forehead and prayed for me together, making sure I didn't feel alone as the nurses put up a sheet between us and the doctor. Josh took one look over the curtain, saw my stomach wide open, and he threw up. Handing him my barf bag, the nurses put him in a chair and rolled him out of the room. Just a few seconds later, the doctor pulled the baby out, and poor Josh missed seeing his first child— Gannon Dewayne McKee—born. I hadn't seen Gannon yet, but my mom's eyes were sparkling, and Josh was smiling ear-to-ear through the window.

With a commotion, the doctor realized that Gannon was not breathing, and he started smacking Gannon to get him to breathe. Within minutes, Gannon was screaming, and we all breathed a sigh of relief. In the meantime, I slowly realized that I was unable to breathe and about to pass out, but I was paralyzed from the epidural and couldn't say anything. The hospital messed up and gave me too much medication in the epidural because the dose is based on height and weight, and they thought I was taller than four foot nine. As a result, the epidural began to paralyze my lungs. I stopped breathing and technically died. When I came to, my doctor had two fingers shoved in my inner jaw to check for a pulse. Josh and my mom had no clue because they were in the other room paying attention to what was going on with the baby. It was so scary, and I remember thinking that this was it. The baby was good, but I was going to die. I told my mom the next day at the hospital that it had happened and how weird it was. She marched out like a mama bear and started asking the nurse questions. The nurse said, "Well, yes, that did happen, but we didn't tell you about it because she's fine now." Thank goodness we were just happy to all be alive with a chubby, healthy baby.

Even though I was exhausted, I was overjoyed when the nurse came in with my son for the first time. "Nine pounds, seven ounces, and twenty inches long," the nurse said, handing him to me. Up until this moment, I had imagined hundreds of times that the baby would look like me. I couldn't wait to see my "mini-me," but then they handed me an exact copy of Josh. And from that moment on, I was so in love. He had a huge head of black hair and shiny brown eyes, and he was so fat that he could barely even open his eyes. The most surprising thing was that he had so much hair all over his big baby body that he looked like a little grizzly bear! If you look at the picture of me holding him for the first time, he already looked half my size, and I'm so tiny that I look like a child holding a baby! When they handed him to me, I melted and felt the biggest rush of love and warmth I have ever experienced in my life. It was like a drug! He was so perfect, and I was obsessed with every square inch of his body. I will never forget holding Gannon that first time and thinking, *"How could I experience this kind of love at the age of sixteen?"*

My mom was in the surgery room with me, so she was there to hold him for the first time. As soon I could, I was telling everyone about the new love of my life, Gannon Dewayne McKee.

One thing that really helped was that Josh had his Native card from being Cherokee, and since the baby was also Cherokee Native American, he also would have his card and most of my pregnancy would be covered financially. As teenage parents with no money, we were so thankful to have this assistance, and I have no idea how we would have afforded it otherwise.

After a few days, it was time to go home, and I vividly remember leaving the hospital with my parents and Josh. Our town is so tiny, so you always know what's going on, and on this particular Friday night, there was a caravan going on for the football game. All my high school friends were lined up with their cars, driving and honking, music blaring. We passed a bus full of cheerleaders and football players hyping themselves up for the big game. That moment hit me like a brick wall, it was a huge wake-up call that my life was going to be different from here on.

Fairly quickly after Gannon was born, I started feeling better and stronger every day. I was so eager to get back to school and cheer. Even though I was thrilled to be a new mom, I knew that getting back to school would be good for my mental health, as well as the future I could give Gannon and myself.

All the pregnant girls and teenage mothers in my area enrolled in an alternative school in order to study and take care of their kids, but I decided to stay at my own school, which was pretty unheard of at the time. Sometimes the workload was overwhelming, but thank goodness I have so much energy and determination. All night, I would nurse Gannon, and in the morning, I took him to daycare before heading off to cosmetology school. When those classes were done, I got on the bus and went to regular school before picking Gannon up at the end of the day. After getting him settled at home, I went to work, took him over to Josh's house, or went to cheer at football and basketball games. Looking back, I have no idea how I did it all! But I do know that my mom was the reason I was able to do all of it because she helped me take care of Gannon whenever she could. She was always there for him—and me. I was so lucky to have her unwavering support. There's just no way I could have done this all without her, and I am eternally grateful for that.

Another thing I'm so grateful that my mom did was she encouraged me to get back to school as quickly as I could. She made sure to tell me often that I was a "somebody" and that I didn't have to let having a baby at sixteen years old define me. "This didn't ruin you," she told me. "You're not just 'the girl who got pregnant in high school,' Mickey." I appreciated her support so much because when it seemed like the rest of the world was against me, she stayed right by my side and held my hand.

It seemed like a simple decision to go back to school to finish my education and participate in activities, but initially, the community seemed to have other opinions about what I should and should *not* be allowed to do. Parents at the school were livid, even some of the cheer squad parents. They didn't want a teen mom on the squad. It wasn't like I was bringing my baby to sit on the sidelines while I cheered at basketball games, but I guess they thought just the fact that people knew I had a baby would be damaging to the school. There was constant chatter about me, and I could feel the eyes of the other congregation members burning a hole through me as they stared when I attended services with Gannon. It felt like no one wanted me to be a happy mom. I made a mistake by having sex and getting pregnant before marriage, and because of that, they felt I should be punished for as long as possible. I certainly shouldn't be living my life without paying some kind of personal price. Never mind that I was juggling school, work, and parenthood with little money, as well as the ups and downs of my diabetes. Why couldn't I live a normal and happy life despite the mistakes I had made? It hurt to feel that kind of rejection, mostly from adults, especially when I was trying to do all the right things and learn from my mistakes.

I wanted to be the best mom, student, teammate, and daughter I could be, but so many people abandoned me in my time of need, and it was confusing and hard to go through at such a young age.

There was no way I was giving up, though. I'd been through so much, and I wasn't about to quit school or stop going to church when I knew that both were good for Gannon and me. One of my best friends would even eat lunch in the bathroom stall with me so I could pump milk for baby Gannon. The school didn't allow me a time or room for this, so I did as my mom taught me by straightening my crown and figuring it out. Eventually, my true friends showed themselves, and most of the cheer squad's parents came around. Strangely, I started tumbling better than I ever had after I had Gannon! I lost the pregnancy weight in two weeks, and within five weeks, I had a six-pack! My teammates started coming over to my house every day, and we'd hang out and play with Gannon. I quickly became obsessed with every little thing he would do. He would yawn, and it was adorable. His coos and gurgles were the highlights of my days. Still, it was incredibly difficult finding myself trying to live a double life, juggling time to be a popular, cool girl while maintaining my little family with Josh.

Sadly, Josh was not fully on board with playing the dad role. He didn't come around very often, and he didn't really show much interest in helping raise Gannon. My mom and I were really the ones who were raising him. Of course, if Josh asked to see Gannon, I'd bring him over to his house, but I didn't understand why he didn't want to be more involved. He ended up missing out on many of those early experiences and milestones that all babies go through.

Taking care of Gannon came so naturally to my mom. He was the first grandchild for my parents, and for years, he was their only grandchild, so you can imagine the attention he received from my family. My mom was obsessed with giving him a good life, and the two hit it off and were the best of friends. During the first months, she and my brother would check on him four times a night to make sure he was sleeping well. She spent all the time she could caring for him, and this created a strong bond between her and Gannon because she was raising him along with me. Come to think of it, since I was still so young, she was really still raising me too. Gannon liked and was much more attached to her than to me, and it really was a gift to see the special bond between the two of them, even though sometimes I would just want him to like me more. We were under her roof, and she was taking care of us both along with the rest of the family. Like the Energizer Bunny, she just never seemed to run out of steam. She just kept going and going, always giving to others and rarely to herself. And she loved being able to take over the aspects of parenting that she loved, such as giving Gannon a bath and rocking him to sleep every night. Being a caregiver came so naturally to her. I think a lot of people wondered why she was helping so much, and that I must have been a neglectful mom or begged her to take over the way she did, but that simply wasn't true. Although I needed the help, she was ALL about Gannon. She just jumped in and did it all. I saw how happy it made her, so sometimes I would sit on the couch and watch her do the nightly routine of bathing and putting him to sleep. We would sit and talk about how special he was to us.

When I reflect on the past, it makes me really sad that Josh wasn't the type of dad that both Gannon and I needed him to be during that first year, but there's just no way that Josh and I could have raised him on our own. I will forever be grateful that my mom set the example and took the lead to show me what a good mom does.

Crowning Achievement:

However we bring children into our lives, whether through a C-section, natural birth, adoption, fostering, or having someone carry the baby, it is a blessing from God. I loved looking at the baby I had just carried, and it gave me joy to realize that God knew Gannon before he was formed and had already set him apart. He, along with every human, is far more special than he could ever realize. God made us all unique, and I was eager to watch my son take on the world with anything his little heart desired.

Chapter 13

WHERE DO WE STAND?

*For they loved the glory that comes from man
more than the glory that comes from God
John 12:43*

The night that my episode of *16 & Pregnant* aired was easily one of the weirdest nights of my life. A few friends came over to support me, and we watched the show with my mom. Even though Josh wasn't too into the show, he watched it at his house with his parents.

Seeing myself on TV was such a strange feeling—it didn't seem real. In just one short hour, I watched my social media following jump from three hundred to three thousand. It was mind-blowing. Things seemed fine until I went to school the next day. The halls were so silent you could hear a pin drop, and as people pointed and whispered, I clung to my friend group feeling like they were all I had. Josh's school was even smaller than mine, maybe a total of thirty students in his grade, and they hated that I had taken someone they loved and exploited him on TV. Word got back to me that people were talking about me in certain classes and that even the teachers were chiming in with their opinions. It was an awful and uncomfortable experience I never expected.

I knew that in a few weeks after the first episode aired, it would be time to travel to New York to film the reunion show with Dr. Drew, and that excitement made things a little easier. It wasn't really the reunion that I was looking forward to; it was the trip to New York City with my mom that I was so happy about. We would probably never have the money to do something like this again. Josh was even allowed to go with us. Neither he nor I had ever even been on a plane before, and we were so excited to experience it together. Interestingly, even though we were having so many "firsts" together, this would not be our first stay together in a hotel room. In fact, because we weren't married, Josh had his own room, and my mom and I shared another. I honestly loved being with my mom, though, and I know Josh enjoyed that time alone.

Just being in New York was like a dream come true, but Josh and I had no idea that my mom had practically every minute of free time already planned out for us. When 7:00 AM rolled around that first morning, I assumed we would sleep in because this felt like a vacation, but NOPE! She forced me out of bed and even had my clothes picked out for me because she was not wasting time. We went to Josh's room and knocked and knocked. When he didn't answer, we tried calling his cell, but still no answer. Our last attempt was having the MTV security guard call his room to check on him. What was Josh doing? He was passed out sound asleep, because apparently, he had stayed up late, buying $299 worth of steaks and movies at 2:00 AM the night before. When we finally got through to him, all my mom had to say was, "Get your butt up, son! We're in New York, and we have things to do!" She was not about to waste a minute of this trip.

While the rest of the cast and their families chilled at the hotel, my mom had our one whole free day in the city completely mapped out for us. We walked through Times Square, and her eyes lit up with how amazing this place was. This place that, up until that day, we had only ever seen on TV. In the midst of all the bright flashing lights, my mom and I held hands and jumped up and down screaming when a commercial for *16 & Pregnant* came on, and there was my pregnant belly right in the middle of Times Square!

Next, we strolled through Central Park—one place that she wanted to tell people she had visited. Then we took a subway (something we never had done) to Ground Zero and saw where the Twin Towers had once stood, and overwhelming emotions flowed through us as we remembered the sadness of what happened on 9/11. It was surreal standing in the very place where so many had lost their lives. Finally, we took a ferry out to see the Statue of Liberty before returning to our hotel right at bedtime. Josh and I still look back and laugh, because we know that had it just been us, we would have 100 percent stayed in the same room and made bad choices, not going one single place she took us to. She was a ball full of energy, and we barely kept up.

The next day, we filmed the reunion with twelve of us *16 & Pregnant* girls. It was super fun to meet them all and good to be away from my hometown for a while to just clear my head. Right before I went on stage, my palms were sweaty, and my blood sugar began to drop. I honestly couldn't believe this was real life. My mom came over to pray with me, and this caused quite a few stares, but she didn't care. Then, she winked at me and said, "Go get 'em, tiger." It always seemed to work back then, because when I hit that cheer mat and saw thousands of people in a crowd, it was my time to shine. But at that moment, it did not strike any luck my way. I sat on the stage with a huge smile, looking like a deer in the headlights. Dr. Drew asked if I was okay and why I smiled so much when my life was figuring out how to care for a baby while I was still a baby. My only answer was, "My mom taught me to smile through life," and when I walked off stage, I buried my head in my arms and felt like the biggest idiot in the world.

When it was time for Josh and me to go back onstage together, Dr. Drew had nothing good to say about him. It was not a good relationship with the two of them from the start. Dr. Drew seemed to favor the moms of the show, because he frequently called out the men for their poor behavior and parenting, but he didn't call out the women to the same degree. It was the same for Josh and me, and instead of defending himself by calling out what I had done wrong, Josh chose to keep quiet and protect my reputation. He had to sit and listen while Dr. Drew questioned his commitment to Gannon and me. My mom sat on the couch on stage beside us and did her best to just hold us through it all. After all this drama, you can imagine how surprised we were when we got back to our hotel and I saw a text from MTV asking if my mom, Josh, and I would like to stay a few extra days with some of the other girls from the show. My mom squealed and clapped her hands. She *loved* New York City, but we were all curious as to why we were asked. The next day when we all met again, they asked the big question—"Can we continue to follow your story?" As anger visibly began boiling up in Josh's face, I thought about how he never talked much to me about his feelings or told me no. And I didn't care what he thought—this was something I couldn't say no to. I calmly said yes to the producer, and as I walked away holding my mom's hand, we were stunned. Squeezing each other's hands, she said, "Sis, they like us!" I barely slept that night and had no clue what was ahead of me, but one thing was certain. The more I was in the spotlight, the more Josh wanted to distance himself.

Shortly after, filming continued during the first season of *Teen Mom 3*. Once again, I started to feel like I was losing my sense of self. I wasn't as humble as I should have been the more my name got out there, and I'd look for ways to do things just to get myself talked about for more attention and fame. Josh told me that I was changing, and it bothered him, but I loved being in the spotlight. I told him I would go ahead and do whatever I wanted, regardless of whether it irritated him.

I was so excited that so many people connected with me and my story, and I hoped that I could find some way to ride this little bit of fame for a while.

After the show came out, Josh and I started really drifting apart and going our separate ways. I was getting more and more disappointed with Josh, and I had no idea in which direction I should go. I went from "I'm so crazy in love with this guy" to "He is nothing." Things had gotten pretty bad between us, and he just wasn't there for us. Josh, on the other hand, said that he didn't want to be around me. He thought that now all I wanted was to be famous and the center of attention. I'm not going to lie—my head had gotten a little too big for my crown, and even though I was holding my head up high, everyone could see how poorly my crown now fit. Josh was so fed up that his small-town girlfriend thought she was some kind of princess since being on TV. I was no longer the little country blonde he had fallen in love with.

It's true that I probably became a little too preoccupied with being on TV, but I didn't have much else going for me. Sure, I was finishing school, but things with Josh were so rough. He wasn't trying to have a family with me. I wanted a house for us, but that was the last thing on his mind. He wasn't working toward anything, and our relationship seemed to be disintegrating before my eyes. He was immature and not ready for a kid, and even though I understood that, it wasn't right. Most teenagers are not ready for such a huge step like parenthood, but we made the decision together to have and raise this baby, and I wanted both of us to be equally committed. I was working, finishing school, raising the baby, and going out, but I still found time to be with Gannon. I loved him with all my heart and wanted to be around him all the time. The fact that Josh just wasn't there was so hurtful. There was a while when my mom was disappointed in him and didn't think I should be with him anymore, even though they had loved Josh from day one.

During this time, it was extremely difficult sticking things out with Josh. Fans who watched the show began noticing that he really didn't show me any emotion or affection. In his defense, Josh is very old-fashioned, but he wouldn't even hold my hands or get close to me in front of our friends when we weren't even being filmed, because he thinks it's trashy and uncomfortable to do that in front of others. He was affectionate behind closed doors, and he was 100 percent a better person when the TV cameras weren't rolling and focused on us. It was pretty clear from the start that he didn't really have a TV personality, and that often made him look like a loser on the show, which wasn't entirely fair. He is still a very shy and private person, but he's not the jerk that people on

TV think he is. I've always told him that if he would just act like himself when we're filming, America would fall in love with him and see all the great things that I love about him. In fact, when people meet him after knowing him only from TV, the first thing they usually notice is what a good guy he is and how much he loves me. But because he seems so closed off on TV, fans often remark that he can't be the "right one" for me. At times when he was absent during those first months with Gannon, I had to agree with them.

Because we were fighting a lot, sometimes Josh would just stop talking to me, and I wouldn't know if we were still together or not. On the weekends after I put Gannon to bed, I'd go out and party with my friends, because if Josh didn't want to be with me, at least they did. As a result, I made quite a few bad decisions during this phase of my life when I felt conflicted about the future of my relationship with Josh. I also had Gannon to think about now, and I didn't want him to see his parents at odds with each other all the time.

Things got so bad, that when I was off at cheer camp, Josh and his friends got into some trouble with a trampy group of drunk girls. Word got back to me about Josh getting close to one of the girls from this group, and the first thing I did was go to this girl's boyfriend and tell him what had happened. He was thankful I told him, and he asked if I wanted to meet up with him the next day. I was ready to show his wife and Josh that if you mess with me, I will get you back ten times worse. *And I did!* I started hanging out with her husband! Real classy, right?

Surprisingly, guys were not scared away from dating me even though I had a kid. But every time I tried to date someone else, somehow Josh and I would find our way back to each other. We'd make up, fight, take a break, and get back together constantly.

Things were obviously not perfect, and I felt like I was turning into some crazy girl who was acting completely out of character. His friends started making fun of me and saying I was psycho, so I tried backing off and doing my own thing with friends or talking to other guys to save myself from more humiliation. After the show aired, I always had to keep the possibility of someone overhearing me or watching me in the back of my head. High school drama was no longer just that—it was people in my town running to the tabloids now.

One of the worst decisions I made during this time was calling up my ex again. It wasn't that I was in love or still pining away for him, but I knew he would be there if I asked him to. If Josh didn't want me, my ex would nearly always come and try to help me pick up the pieces of my broken heart. And, since my ex and Josh were friends, it didn't hurt that the word would absolutely get back to Josh that my ex and I were hanging out again. I hoped that would really get under his skin.

Once I started seeing my ex again, people in Josh's life started telling him to give up on me. They'd say, "She doesn't want you, bro. She doesn't love you. She's cheating on you again—get away from her." Even though I didn't really know where our relationship stood at the moment, in the back of my head, all I wanted was my little family with Josh. I wanted the perfect life I envisioned, but instead, we let so many things come between us that soured our love for one another. The show had a lot of the blame for coming between us, because as much as I loved the attention, Josh still hated the effect that even just a little bit of fame had on me. All of a sudden, I was getting noticed and starting to get a little more independent. We still didn't have much money, but I wanted to pursue opportunities coming my way if they might give us a better life. If it were up to Josh, though, he would have us stay home all the time and be content because that would make us depend on each other more. In his eyes, that meant we would grow closer, but that's not the way I wanted to live.

I had to admit that even though we had more downs than ups at this time, I hated the thought of Josh dating someone else. We had been engaged and then broken up so many times before, and honestly, this roller coaster ride was getting old. I was exhausted from trying to figure out where we stood with each other from day to day, so when we ran into each other one night, I was surprised how easy it still was for us to laugh and have fun together. It felt like the first days of our relationship again, and I loved it. We were talking about how we had something special, and that we should just get back together for good and finally get married—not plan a wedding or anything—just get married. In my heart of hearts, I really wanted to get married and finally settle down and be a real family.

Crowning Achievement:

I was falling fast into the trap of craving acceptance from people and falling away from the glory that comes from God, and believe me when I say that this was a slap in the face. I hate the way I acted when I first came into the spotlight. Life has a crazy way of teaching us lessons, and I'm sure glad I was able to learn from this one.

Chapter 14

SHOTGUN WEDDING

Be completely humble and gentle; be patient,
bearing with one another in love.
Ephesians 4:2

Josh offered to drive me home from that night after we re-kindled, and I decided it would be a good opportunity for some serious talk. I told him that we either needed to make this relationship work now or leave each other forever. After I was done spilling my heart, Josh looked over at me and calmly said, "If you want to get married, come pick me up tomorrow morning and be dressed."

I couldn't believe it, but he just kept saying the same thing over and over. "Come over and be dressed if you want to get married tomorrow." Not really believing he was being serious,

I told him I'd be there at 9:00 AM and he had better be ready when I got there.

When I finally got to bed late that night, the reality of what we discussed set in. Were we really going to get married tomorrow? I mean, I could wear my graduation dress, I supposed. I had no money to buy a real wedding dress, and besides, where would I get a wedding dress with no notice? The dress that my mom had bought for me to wear to my high school and cosmetology school graduation a month earlier would have to do. I'd only worn it once, and it happened to be white. That seemed like my only option. I went to bed with my head still spinning about all the possibilities that tomorrow could bring.

With little sleep, I got up early and put on my white dress. I texted Josh to ask him how I should wear my hair, because, after all, I wanted to look as pretty as possible for him if we were really going to go through with this. We'd remember this day forever, so I wanted it to feel right. Josh told me to wear my hair down and curly with a flower in it—just the way he liked it. When I think back to that day, I can't get over that I put little flower clippies in my hair for my wedding. That's how young I was! When I walked out of my room all dressed at 9:00 AM, my mom looked a little startled.

"Where in the world are you going so early looking like that?" she asked. I told her that Josh and I were going on a morning date, and I still can't believe she bought that, because that story didn't make any sense at all. It's not like I'd ever gone out on a date looking like that—especially at 9:00 AM! She said I could use her car, so I jumped in and sped off nervously to Josh's house.

As I parked in the driveway, he stepped out onto his front porch. He was quite a sight in his polished cowboy boots, belt buckle, button-up shirt, and cowboy hat. At that very moment, it finally dawned on me. "Oh my gosh. We are really doing this!" Smiling from ear to ear, Josh jumped in the passenger seat, and we headed toward the courthouse.

On the way there I recall saying, "Josh, do you really want to do this? *Now* it's getting serious. If you want to back out, let's not do this. I don't want to if you're just doing it because you think it's the right thing to do." Honestly, at that moment, I would not have been surprised to hear him say that we should turn around and go back home. All of this seemed so spontaneous and a little ridiculous, but I've never been a planner. If I wanted something, I would just go after it. But I wanted to make sure his heart was really in it, because I couldn't bear the thought of him only doing this because he thought it was what I wanted. I needed to know that he cared and was truly committed to giving this marriage a shot.

He turned to me, grabbed my hand, and said, "I want to spend the rest of my life with you." Hearing those words and seeing the intense look in his eyes was all it took to convince me as we pulled up to the courthouse. He honestly appeared to be ready and willing to take this jump with me, and I loved that he didn't have a second thought about it. We both felt ecstatic as we jumped out of the car.

We walked into the courthouse and put our money together to buy the license. Then, we walked across the street to a tiny chapel where a minister (who had to have been at least 150 years old) was waiting to marry us. Before we stepped into the chapel, I told myself one more time not to be stupid—maybe this was just what *I* wanted and not what Josh wanted. "If you have any doubt, let's not go in," I begged him.

He looked at me again in that serious way I had only seen a few minutes earlier. "This is 100 percent what I want," he insisted, and he grabbed my hand as we took our first steps into the chapel together. One thing I have always loved about Josh is that he *always* wanted to be my husband. When I see friends beg men for years to simply slap a ring on their finger, I am thankful that I have a man who would marry me over and over again. I hoped that this service wasn't going to take too long, because this poor old minister standing at the front behind the pulpit looked like he was barely hanging on to life. My heart was racing, and I was ready to get this started.

Josh looked so deeply into my eyes and repeated the vows word for word. I was shaking because I was so nervous and scared, but he seemed so calm and sure of everything, and that comforted me. I finally said my vows, and we sealed the moment with a kiss—a beautiful, long, close moment with Josh holding the back of my head toward him as he embraced me.

After what seemed like an eternity of holding one another there in the chapel, we finally came back down to Earth. "Holy cow!" I said. "We did it! We really did it! Oh, crap—we'd better go tell everyone now!" Now that we had made it official, we wanted to tell the world! Since it was just the old man and us, we gave him my camera and begged him to snap a photo so we could always remember this moment before we told the world. We left the chapel, ran back into the car, and headed back to Josh's house.

We immediately went inside Josh's house and told his parents, and his mom snapped a group picture of all of us right there in the living room so we could remember this day. We hugged and shed a few tears before taking off to give the news to my parents.

Literally, all I said to my parents when we stepped into their house was, "Mom and Dad, we have something to tell you," before my mom screamed, "You didn't get *married*, did you?" She just knew that something was different between Josh and me—she could see and feel it. My mom asked the question any other parent would. "Why the rush?" she wondered. "We could have planned a wedding!"

But remember, Josh and I didn't exactly do anything the "right way" in life, so why not add getting married to that list of madness? She sat in shock for a while, but I stayed patient, as her opinion mattered most to me. Josh had asked my dad long ago for his blessing for the day our wedding would come, but they had no idea that today would be that day.

After more hugs, tears, and laughs, my mom threw her hands up and turned to Josh with a serious look in her eyes. She looked at me before turning back to him. "Okay, Josh. It's time you both give your marriage to God and put Him first. It's time that you two stop all the fighting now." She also said that she had been praying for her children's future spouses every single day for years—even before she knew them. "I'm going to treat you both the same," she continued. "You are both my children now, and I'm not going to take sides. I will call you both out when I think you need it." Josh felt so lucky to have my parents as in-laws, and they said they'd root for us no matter what. They were as committed to our marriage as we were, and it was a blessing to feel that kind of love and support.

One of the best things about our wedding night is that my mom *finally* let us sleep in the same bed together, so Josh stayed the whole night at my house. I never wanted to live with him before we were married, but now we could have sleepovers! That was our "honeymoon"—*a sleepover at my parents' house*! All the same, that first night we spent together—our wedding night—was very romantic and full of love. It was such an exciting step, and we were taking it together, hand in hand. That night was so wonderful, in fact, that I've done the math and promise you that was the very night I got pregnant for the second time.

Crowning Achievement:

Josh and I knew nothing about love, or life in general, when we got married. We never even opened our Bibles first to read what God expected from us as a married couple. We just knew we loved one another, but I now know that I would have been a better wife if I would have dug into God's word first. Love is so many things—patient, humble, and kind—and when two become one, it is a *huge* commitment. I hope others will approach it more seriously and cautiously than I did, and one of the best places to start is being prepared in Christ before jumping into marriage.

Chapter 15

WEDDING PART 2

*Train up a child in the way he should go; even
when he is old he will not depart from it.*
Proverbs 22:6

The plan after our shotgun wedding was that Josh and I would live at my parents' house and raise Gannon. I was accepted to college and made the cheer squad. I was super excited that my dreams of college cheerleading were coming true, and I could not wait to start cheer camp to prepare for the upcoming football season. Being in college, though, was probably not the best environment for a young married mother. My friends, single and child-free, were partying every chance they could get. Every weekend, we were invited to house parties where a lot of drinking and wildness took place. Not wanting to miss out on the college experience, I went along with my friends. Josh was not the jealous type, nor was he one to investigate (unlike me).

A month after our shotgun wedding and right after starting college, I found out I was pregnant again. My heart was shattered, because I didn't want to be the one on the cheer squad who couldn't go to practice and cheer at games again. I continued to go to practices while I still could, but after a few months of pregnancy, I broke my foot and couldn't get around campus anymore, so I quit. Of course, I was disappointed that I couldn't stick it out and make my college dreams come true, but I had to think that maybe this was God's way of protecting me and my relationship with Josh. Undoubtedly, I would have gone on to make some bad decisions if I had stuck it out and kept up the college lifestyle. You become who you're around, and I was constantly around a wild bunch of kids. Yes, I was having tons of fun with them, but there's no way I would have stayed with Josh if I had stayed in college. There were too many distractions and temptations. Instead, I stayed at home, prepared for baby number two, and taught myself how to crochet.

Three months into my pregnancy, I told Josh that I wanted a real wedding—and a big one too. He really didn't want that, but he played along. Our little chapel wedding was perfect for Josh. It was private, quiet, and romantic. He is such a real person and doesn't care what other people think, and I believe that wedding meant a lot to him. The vows seemed so real and so honest, and I don't think he had ever looked at me like he did that day. He was just so happy as he said his vows to now have Gannon and me forever.

I, however, wanted the world to know and the world to see me marry the man I loved. I was too selfish to let Josh take the lead and make that our only wedding. I wanted my way. I wish I could go back and appreciate our little wedding and see it more as a special moment, but at the time, all I wanted was to wear a pretty dress, have pictures, and dance in a barn. I got busy planning a big wedding, but I don't think Josh really cared for any of it. He preferred our first wedding because it seemed more intimate, sincere, and genuine, and that was more than enough for him. He was willing to go through a fancy wedding since I wanted one and didn't like to take "no" for an answer. Just like with TV, he just didn't want all eyes on him, so you can probably guess how he felt when MTV called and asked to film our wedding for *Teen Mom 3.* They wanted it to be part of the season, and while I was thrilled, Josh was not.

I was so excited for our big wedding because it was turning out to be exactly the kind of celebration I had always imagined. I walked down the aisle in the perfect bedazzled white dress and cowgirl boots with all my friends by my side. Josh, all dressed up in his cowboy clothes, danced with me all night. It was amazing sharing all the happiness and fun with our families and friends.

While we were dancing, Josh leaned down and whispered into my ear, "Want to go to an amusement park and stay in a hotel tonight?" We were so poor, but he wanted me to feel like I had a honeymoon, so I hugged him tight, excited to get away together to Branson, Missouri. To us, spending a couple hundred bucks was a lot of money, but this was special. We even invited our friends to join us in riding roller coasters. We rode so many and then bought a funnel cake. After the ups and downs of the coasters and the greasy food, we felt nothing less than unpleasant as we walked back to our cars. On the way back to the hotel, we went to a Chinese food drive-through and got our favorite food, but we were so sick from the roller coasters that we barely made it. Every time we go to Branson, Missouri, we still eat at this same special Chinese place and laugh about the time we got so sick on the roller coasters.

After we got married, it was like a switch went off all of a sudden for Josh. He wanted to be Gannon's best buddy, and he was doing all he could to be a better dad. When Josh started getting more involved, it was hard for my mom to give up her role as a stand-in parent for Gannon. She had raised him when Josh wasn't around, and now, she felt Josh was trying to take Gannon away from her. They also had very different parenting styles that would sometimes clash. Josh would put him in the corner, and my mom would go sneak him out. She felt she had the right to do that because she raised him when Josh was not. It put me in an awkward spot, too, because I saw both sides. Josh was saying, "Hey, that is my son. I know I wasn't the best, but now I'm an adult and want to be this kid's dad." But my mom was heartbroken that she was losing opportunities to be involved in raising Gannon.

Josh and I made the very difficult decision to move out with Gannon and into a place of our own, because it felt like the right thing to do as newlyweds and parents. Of course, my mom accepted that and understood that our marriage was taking a step in the right direction, but she cried when we left. I know she shed tears for sadness, but I'm also positive that some of those tears were for the pride she felt in Josh as he stood up and tried to right the wrongs he made early on as a father. Since then, he's been the best dad I could ever have asked for in someone, and he has been very honest about his mistakes during that first year of Gannon's life. He has apologized so many times, and the good heart-to-heart talks he has had with Gannon since have gone a long way in making up for that time they both lost out on.

Crowning Achievement:

Raising kids is not easy. I had a kid while still figuring out who I was, and moving forward from that has been a real challenge. Today I strive to raise each child to love God and understand how important they are to this world. How we raise these children in their upbringing is so important.

Chapter 16

JAXIE TAYLOR

Behold, children are a heritage from the Lord,
the fruit of the womb a reward.
Psalms 127:3

Even though we'd taken some significant steps forward in marrying and moving out on our own, Josh and I found ourselves having a hard time figuring life out now with some money and two children. While he was over the moon that we were having a girl, I was disappointed. We were married, living together, and Josh was treating me well, but he didn't understand why I wasn't super thrilled to have this girl. Of course, I would love any baby that was ours, but deep down, I did not want a girl. I think it had a lot to do with the trauma I went through when I was so young, and I didn't know if I could protect a daughter from those kinds of damaging experiences. To be honest, I also didn't want to end up raising a little firecracker like myself, since I was such a pain to raise and caused my mom and dad a lot of headaches.

Just like with Gannon, I had to schedule a C-section because our daughter was going to be too big for me to deliver naturally, even though it was still a month before my due date. Big babies are a trademark of mothers with type 1 diabetes, so I sure was living up to that stereotype.

Jaxie Taylor McKee was born on February 7, 2014. She weighed eight pounds, eleven ounces and was nineteen inches long. When she arrived, I remember that the nurse handed her to Josh to hold first. He was beaming from ear to ear, holding her close and kissing her. He didn't want anyone else touching his perfect baby girl.

My mom took a deep breath and looked at us as a couple and said, "Okay, I guess I will leave now. Call me if you need me." It was obvious that she wanted to stay so badly, because her baby now had a second baby! When Gannon was born, she stayed by Josh's and my side the entire first week. She got so attached to Gannon and helped us through it all. This time, however, she knew we needed to learn how to be adults on our own, but I could still tell it was hard for her to go.

When she left, Josh looked over at me and was surprised and concerned to see that I was not reacting with the same joy that he was. When Gannon was born, I just melted as I held him against my skin for the first time. Gannon was my whole world, my whole life, my pride and joy, and I just couldn't imagine loving someone more.

Because I wasn't eagerly reaching out to hold Jaxie, Josh kept asking me what was wrong. She was so healthy and beautiful, and he didn't understand why I didn't look happy. I told him I was just letting him have his time with her.

Josh said, "You don't like her? Why don't you like her?"

"Of course, I like her," I assured him, but he wanted more proof.

"Hold her—kiss her. Give her a kiss," he begged me, searching for any sign that I was smitten as he was with her. When he finally handed her to me, a flood of emotions ran through my body—almost too many for me to handle. My entire world had just changed once again. I couldn't believe it—I had a daughter! I was going to be raising a baby girl. Holding her made me realize I had just met my forever best friend, and the room was filled with magic. I had a lump in my throat as I stared at this perfect little angel in my arms. I was so incredibly proud to be her mom. Not only that, but I couldn't wait for Gannon to meet his new baby sister.

Jaxie is such an amazing child, and each day she surprises me with her sweet personality and attitude. She is the complete opposite of both Josh and me. She is a true daddy's girl, and Josh loves that he has a little princess to protect. I am certain that if a man ever touches her, that's when Josh will end up in prison, because there's no way he will let anyone hurt her. She has him wrapped around her finger. Her heart is huge, and she is always happy for others. She is not competitive or envious of anyone and always says sorry for anything she thinks she might have done, unlike me. The fact alone that she says sorry makes her so different from me! Honesty, kindness, and gentleness just come naturally for her, and it's a wonderful thing to experience as her mom.

Another thing that I love about Jaxie is that she is more content with what she has, and she isn't as driven as I am. I enrolled her in cheer, and she just didn't have the will to do it. Instead of being upset or disappointed, watching her just made me laugh. I thought it was hilarious that she just didn't care or have a competitive bone in her body. Her sweet and pure nature is a gift from God and has completely put my fears of raising a girl to rest.

The next few months were a turning point in our marriage. *Teen Mom 3* was canceled after just one season, and even though I was sad that we weren't going to be on TV anymore, things were starting to feel better again between Josh and me, and he was clearly happier that our little family was living a more normal life together now. He fell in love with me *before* TV, and then he fell out of love with me because of the person I became *on* TV. He felt that after TV, I always wanted more and was never happy enough or content with what we had.

But I was still choosing the spotlight over him. He doesn't see any good in fame, and he only wanted me. I, however, wanted both Josh and TV, and I tried to see his perspective, but it took me a long time to understand his viewpoint. It was a big step for me to even see his side of things because I wasn't always like that. Usually, I wanted things my way and didn't care about what Josh thought, but I had to really stop and learn how to be more considerate of his perspective.

We've both been through so much and practically grew up together on TV. People have seen our ups and downs, and I've been very open and honest about our problems. He has never gone on social media or told the tabloids what I've done to him, but I've told everything he has done to me. Josh hates that. I always tried to be a good wife behind the cameras, but I put him through so much that he didn't want to go through.

In many ways, I don't think, though, that I could be where I am today without Josh. He still has so much patience and grace with me, and I'm certain that no other man would have put up with so much from me. My mom agreed that was why Josh and I were meant to be together—because no one else would give me as much freedom to be my true self. He used to have anger problems, but he has never hurt me. He's punched holes in the walls and had a drinking problem, but you can't make him mad even if you tried. I could say the worst thing ever to him, and he would just say, "Love you," because he knows it's just petty, and there's no point in getting mad.

But if I do something that bothers him, he won't even tell me, and he'll just get over it in his own way. I'm so stubborn that I really need someone like Josh—completely uncontrolling and patient with me. I'm going to do it my own way, and if you don't like it, I'll show you the door. That's just my personality. I think that's why my mom always fought for us as a couple. She said that Josh and I together just made sense, and she didn't think there was another man out there who would put up with all my crap. Maybe it's a control issue from my childhood, but I don't want anyone telling me I have to ask permission to spend money. Even if I couldn't control what happened to me, I *could* control other aspects of my life. Over the years, many people have been upset with my mother because they couldn't understand why she wanted us to stick it out. However, she has been the one human on this Earth who knows the ins and outs of my marriage. She knows Josh's heart and the forgiveness he has given me.

Crowning Achievement:

Children are so precious and special to God. We are given a very delicate and huge role when we bring them into this world. I believe it is not our job to shelter them from this cruel world, but to teach them how to live in it, remaining kind to everyone and humble in their ways.

Chapter 17

FAME ISN'T ALWAYS YOUR FRIEND

*Do not love the world or the things in the world. If anyone loves
the world, the love of the Father is not in him. For all that is in the
world—the desires of the flesh and the desires of the eyes and
pride in possessions—is not from the Father but is from the world.*
1 John 2:15-16

After Jaxie was born, we struggled with money. Josh worked every day from 6:00 AM to 5:00 PM (sometimes later) for a drywall company owned by a family friend I'd known since childhood. I got him the job, and this man still to this day is a huge blessing to him. He taught Josh everything he knows about handiwork and has been like a second dad to him.

Meanwhile, I tapped into my social media following and learned how to crochet in an attempt to sell my crocheted items. Because we shared a car, I let Josh drive to work while I scraped up enough money to purchase a bike from Walmart for eighty-nine dollars. It had a basket, and I'd wake up each morning, crochet, and ride my bike to the post office to drop off packages to ship out. Then, I'd bike to Walmart and get more yarn and whatever groceries I could afford. This allowed me to get some human interaction before going back home, nursing Jaxie, and crocheting some more.

I was extremely unhappy with how much we struggled. We had a rental house that was broken into while Josh and I were on a Valentine's Day date. Jaxie was just two weeks old, and all of her baby things were stolen. After that, we decided it wasn't safe for me to be alone there all day, so we moved back in with my mom. Josh was still riding in rodeos on the weekends, so I would take the kids and we'd cheer him on. I was so depressed being home every day. Crocheting wasn't what I wanted my future to be, so I thought about putting the kids in daycare and going back to work in a salon.

MTV had decided they were done with telling the stories from my group of girls on *Teen Mom 3,* and the series was canceled, so I was desperate to find work and support my family. I missed the attention I had from TV and needed something positive in my life, so when I met a producer who sold herself as a "mentor," I thought maybe this would be a chance to get back in the spotlight.

Even though Josh was still reluctant, I wanted to get my name out there and see if I could ride that wave of opportunity a while longer. If I can, I will always want to take the opportunity to turn my recognition into opportunities. You never know what that kind of exposure can do for your life and livelihood. Even after turning my energy into a business, I was still curious about what was out there. That's why I would never succeed at a desk job or having someone else as my boss—I just can't sit still and am always looking for more.

When I was first getting my name out there, it was almost dangerous, as I lost my sense of being humble. I craved things that would get me talked about, no matter what they were, as they brought me attention and more fame. Josh would tell me how much this bothered him, but I was enjoying being in the spotlight, and I would go ahead and do what I wanted, regardless of whether it bothered Josh or my family.

This producer promised she could help me achieve the level of fame and wealth that I wanted so badly if I just trusted her and let her handle boosting my image and relevance. Even though I felt something was a little off, I was willing to take the risk and let her take me under her wing. She was so persuasive and kept coming after me, telling me how great my life could be if I just listened to her.

Well, things got weird quickly. She said she had just the right opportunity for me, and that all I needed to do was let her tell the media that someone "leaked" a sex tape of me. To be clear—there was, *and still is*, NO sex tape. Period. But this producer said that even bad press is good press and that I could go on TV and social media afterward to publicly deny that the tape existed. She convinced me that by doing this, I could turn the experience into speaking engagements for young girls trying to lead better Christian lives. I know. It doesn't make sense in retrospect to me, either, and I don't know why I fell for it. I was young, naive, gullible, and in way over my head. I let my fantasies of a life of fame interfere with who I really was.

I wish my experience with that producer stopped there, but it didn't. I flew to Los Angeles, where she promised that the buzz generated from my visit would spark more career opportunities. She took me to a building in LA and told me she was going to introduce me to a friend. We got out of her car, and her friend was standing outside in front of his business just waiting to greet us. The producer told me to shake the man's hand, and someone snapped a few pictures. Little did I know that I was shaking hands with a famous porn producer and that this was all arranged so she could generate publicity by sending these pictures out to all the tabloids. Here I was, on social media, shaking the hand of a porn king in front of a giant sign with the porn business name emblazoned across it. To seal the deal, the woman told me that now I just needed to "accidentally" send her a picture of my boobs that she could leak to the press, and that's when things would really take off.

There was no way I was going to do that, and she got angry and called the whole deal off. And you know what I got out of it? Absolutely nothing more than a humiliated spouse and family, a long recovery from earning a fake bad reputation, and losing a job as a cheer coach years later because all the moms saw the story on the internet and complained that I was a porn star who wasn't fit to teach kids. At the time, I didn't understand that once something's on the internet, *it never goes away*, and someone will always find it. Rumors run rampant and ruin your name, and I learned the hard way that an opportunity that is going to ruin your name is *not* an opportunity. Keeping your good name is more valuable than any amount of money.

After this disastrous experience, I realized how evil the entertainment industry can be. Other people have more power over your name and image than you do. Some of the other *Teen Mom* girls reached out to me after seeing the story online and told me this industry is evil and to stand my ground so no one would do this to me again,

I'm sure you're thinking, *"How did you let someone take advantage of you like that? What in the world were you thinking?"*

I've had a lot of time to think about this whole fiasco, and what I've realized is that I used to feel so special when someone asked me to do something that I had to say yes. If I was asked to do an interview, I thought that the more I could get my name out there, the more success I would have. I've even been asked during interviews to say whom I hate from *Teen Mom* and what secrets I can tell. In the past, I would have found something bad to say because I felt so special and powerful getting attention and trying to stay relevant. But I don't fall for that trap anymore. Sure, it's important to get my name out there, and the more followers I have, the better my business runs. But I'm not going to get that at the expense of others' reputations and dignities.

I cannot tell you the last time I was able to go to sleep without worrying about what the world is thinking about me. I've often felt humiliated that people know *(or think they know)* every little detail of what's going on in my life. People have perpetuated some pretty terrible rumors about me, and one thing that is important to know is that if I make mistakes or hurt someone, I will always own up to it. When people make false accusations, I don't respond. What's the point? People will continue to believe what they want to believe, and somehow, they'll find something wrong with the way I apologized. I just have to stand tall, know my truth, and hope that people won't believe everything they hear or read about me. It's really hard to be a dartboard for mean people who insist on perpetuating lies about me, but I'm trying to remember that while they may not know my true worth, those who know and love me really do.

Crowning Achievement:

Have you ever heard of someone having all the fame and money in the world but still being depressed and unhappy? It's true. Chasing after worldly possessions is not the key to happiness, and I found that out the hard way. I was so young and easily manipulated, but the more I wanted, the less happy I became. In turn, I made those around me unhappy. I do love working hard and having nice things, yes, but I've learned to be content with and thankful for the life God has given me. The less I chase material items, and the more I fix my eyes on God, the more fulfilled I feel in my heart. It's the humans we are in our lifetime that matters and not the things we own. I will go to my grave with only how rich my heart was.

Chapter 18

EVERY STEP LEADS ME
TO WHERE I BELONG

Count it all joy, my brothers, when you meet trials of various kinds, for you know that the testing of your faith produces steadfastness. And let steadfastness have its full effect, that you may be perfect and complete, lacking in nothing.
James 1: 2–4

A fter that whole mess with the producer, I was hoping to get hired in a big salon, but I was offered a spot in a smaller one and decided to take what I could get at the time since I needed to work. Even then, I knew that being a cosmetologist wasn't really my calling, but I needed the money, and this was the surest way I could make some.

The salon that hired me sat inside a gym. All day, while I was cutting, dyeing, and styling hair, I could see the window that looked out over the gym where several bodybuilders were training for their shows. The owner of the gym was always right in the center of the action, strutting her tan, toned body around the gym and posing in high heels and little else. She was a body-building physique model, and the more I saw her, the more I wanted my shot at that world.

That's when I made up my mind that it was time to spread my wings and grab this opportunity to grow. I was going to try fitness modeling. Even if I failed, it would be a great experience, and I truly believed that every step would lead me to where I belong. I needed some kind of positive inspiration in my life, and I thought this might just be the thing for me. I always feared not even trying far more than I did failing but learning.

Bikini and fitness modeling was a huge stepping-stone for helping me believe in myself. I worked out for several hours a day and did all I could to anticipate what the judges at my next competition would want to see. You never knew, because judges each had their own ideal of what the perfect fitness model would look like, so that made for some unpredictability in the competitions.

Even though I loved reaching for my fitness and health goals, I quickly realized that the fitness modeling industry was full of problems. The industry was crooked and corrupt, and it encouraged women to expect harsh criticism of their bodies and go to extreme measures to attain perfection. It got to the point where I was eating a meager 800 calories per day, when the average recommended calorie intake for women is about 2,000 calories a day. I was starving myself in an attempt to make every square inch of my body look like someone else's ideal.

People at the gym were giving me a lot of praise and attention, telling me my body looked great. But I was anything but strong and healthy on the inside. If I even thought I had an ounce of fat on my body, I would cry and starve myself even more. Other girls I knew, desperate to get their names out there in this industry, had even resorted to using illegal substances to get the look they wanted. It was sickening how willing we all were to go above and beyond to destroy our bodies to look as great in a bikini as we could.

I only trained for a few shows, but my last one was a disaster that caused me to reevaluate what I was doing. After parading around in a tiny bikini and doing poses in front of judges, I was waiting nervously for my results. While my actual scores were acceptable, going over the judges' comments after the competition broke me. The card stated that although my body looked great, I scored low because the back of my arms needed to be toned up. This was heartbreaking to hear because I really couldn't do anything to improve that area. What the judges didn't know was that I had to take my insulin shots in the back of my arms. What they saw as flabby and untoned, were actually "insulin knots," and it's completely normal—expected, even—that little lumps of fat and scar tissue build up there as a result of repeated insulin injections. I would never be able to get rid of those no matter how hard I tried, and I'm sure the judges would never be able to overlook that. I could never fulfill the ultimate bikini bodybuilder's physique. Besides the back of my arms, they also said that I carried too much fat in my butt, and although I could work on that area, Josh said that there was no way he was going to let me get rid of that because he loved the way it looked. At least someone was giving me high scores for my butt!

I have several friends in the industry, and I have nothing bad to say about anyone who chooses this sport. I just don't know if *I* will ever go back to bodybuilding. I know some are able to create a good physique in a more natural way and by putting in the extra work. I just didn't feel it was a healthy choice for me mentally or physically anymore. In the end, I cut my losses and left the industry. I still wanted to do some fitness modeling, but it would have to be something that favors more natural bodies. I also wasn't giving up on doing something with fitness, and more than anything, I was drawn to helping others learn to love themselves and get healthy—especially other moms.

I was excited to move forward with trying to build my own fitness and wellness business, and I even earned my fitness certificate and started doing personal training sessions with clients to begin pursuing this dream. Additionally, another TV network had reached out with an opportunity for me to be on another reality show. Everything was lining up and looking up for me.

Little did I know, but this turned out to be another one of those moments where I thought things were going well, only to have life turn around again and slap me in the face. My period was late, again, and I sent Josh to the drug store to get me a pregnancy test, even though he tried to reassure me that I wasn't pregnant. We had been very safe, and we didn't want another baby. (Well, *I* didn't want another one. Josh would have eight kids with me if my body could handle it.)

I took the test, and Josh read the results to me. "Good," he said. "I *told* you you're not pregnant." I was tired but relieved as I tossed the test in the trash.

A few hours later, I was on a Skype meeting with one of my clients who I was training, and we were talking about what steps we could take to get her body in shape. I was just so excited about fitness—my body looked great and I couldn't wait for others to achieve their fitness goals. One thing the bodybuilding industry did for me was educate me and help me use that knowledge to help others. Josh came into the room during the meeting and said we needed to talk.

"Mackenzie, you need to get off the call," he said with a sense of urgency in his voice. I tried to explain that I was busy with a client, but he just interrupted me again, blurting out, "You're pregnant."

"No, I'm not Josh," I said while trying to cut him off and get back to my client. Turning to look at him, I saw Josh standing there with the pregnancy stick in his hand, and I started shaking. I quickly told the client I had to go, and I felt so unprofessional as I slammed my laptop closed.

"Mackenzie, we didn't wait long enough," Josh said. "I was in the bathroom and dug it out of the trash." Apparently, we hadn't waited long enough before checking the results, and in a rush to get to my meeting, we had misread the results. I was pregnant.

I immediately started crying out of anger. I knew right then and there that my dreams were over. Being pregnant meant no more personal training sessions, no fitness business, and certainly no reality show, as the producers from that show told me from the get-go that I couldn't be pregnant. Turning to Josh, I told him he was the worst person ever and had ruined my life. I had built myself up for this life of fitness, and now I was just going to be pregnant with two children we were already struggling to feed, with no income or home of our own.

I started seeing flashbacks to what a crappy dad Josh had been after Gannon was first born, and I got angrier. I already had two kids with this man. Why in the world should I have another and ruin my dreams again? Seething, I didn't realize how horrible

I was being to Josh, as I refused to look at or even talk to him. Convinced it was all his fault that I was pregnant again, I seemed to forget that it takes two to tango, but I was so devastated and thought blaming Josh would make me feel better about myself.

About a week later, the doorbell rang, and my mom answered the door to find a man handing her a bouquet of flowers. Accepting them, my mom shut the door and turned to me. "You have a really good man in your life, Mackenzie. He loves you."

She handed me the bouquet, and as I read the note attached, I started to cry. The note read: *"I'm so happy to be parents again. I love you, Sugar."* Sugar was a nickname he had always called me.

I rolled my eyes, put the flowers down, and never looked at them again. The flowers just made it worse. This is not what I wanted for my life, and now I was even more upset at Josh for ruining everything in my life. I saw major disappointment in my mother's eyes as she shook her head and walked away. She even placed the flowers on my dresser in a pretty vase in hopes Josh would think I had done it.

That is truly one moment in my life where I wish I could go back. I was so selfish, and in an attempt to hide my disappointment and fear, I lashed out at Josh. When I'm hurt, I show it and talk about it, but Josh doesn't. He holds it all inside, even though he might feel like he's dying inside. Even though he would never say so, I know that my reaction to the pregnancy hurt him deeply.

I was on the right track earlier in this phase of my life when I started working out, fitness modeling, and doing personal training, but I just crashed when I got pregnant. I thought my dream of working in fitness was over, but looking back, all I had to do was have a baby and start a workout program. I could have been much nicer to Josh and just moved forward with my career. Being pregnant is just nine months of life, but I acted as if my world had ended. I could have continued teaching while I was pregnant. It wouldn't have been that big of a deal, but I didn't see that at the time, and I got so depressed because I thought I had lost all I had started to gain. Why was I so awful?

Crowning Achievement:

This was a time that my life took a turn that I didn't want or like. As the book of James says, I should have counted it as joy. It was God's plan for my life, and I wanted something else, so I threw a fit. When we meet trials, it is testing our faith that produces steadfastness. I was searching for how to create the life I wanted for myself, and I was turning away from God when he showed me that was not his plan for me. It's important to find joy in your life changes and remember that good comes out of all hardships once we embrace our challenges.

Chapter 19

ROCK BOTTOM

Cast your burden on the Lord, and he will sustain you;
he will never permit the righteous to be moved.
Psalms 55:22

think God knows that sometimes He has to make me hit rock bottom so I can stand back up. Months later, I was at an all-time low. I was severely depressed and hopeless, and I felt like I had nowhere to turn. Every day was a battle with dark thoughts and emotions. Nothing in me wanted to be alive. One day, I texted Josh that I just didn't want to live anymore. He told my parents, of course, and they were all afraid I was about to make a bad decision.

A few hours after I texted that, I was sitting in my car contemplating the horrible state of my current life. Lost in thought,

I was startled when two police officers started knocking on my driver's side window. They asked my name and told me to get out of the car. I kept asking what was wrong, but instead of giving me an explanation, they handcuffed me on the spot. Suddenly, Josh pulled his car up next to mine, and I couldn't figure out for the life of me why he was there. Then, it dawned on me as he started talking to the police—he was in on this! *He* was the one who had called the cops on me and told them I was threatening to commit suicide. I was livid and started screaming at both Josh and the police.

My emotions were all over the place, and I knew my blood sugar was very high. Luckily, I had my glucometer with me, and when I checked my sugar, it read "HI," which was dangerous and life-threatening. I knew it was a huge reason for my irrational behavior. I looked down at my almost eight-month pregnant belly and suddenly got scared for the baby. I pleaded with the cops to let me go home by telling them I wasn't going to hurt myself. I tried explaining that I'm a diabetic and I could die without my insulin shots, but they completely ignored me and handcuffed me before throwing me in the back seat.

The next thing I knew, the cops were taking me to the hospital prepping to take me to a mental health institution. Sadly, the more I screamed for medical attention, the more the cops sat around in a circle in the hospital room and laughed. I couldn't believe it. It had now been three hours at the hospital and the cop came to tell me my "crazy" husband was at the door trying to get me out. They walked away laughing instead of letting Josh in.

Finally, I let out the biggest scream of my life, *"Someone give me insulin now or my baby will die!"* The cops stood up and slammed me down on a bed nearby. One had a hand over my mouth to shut me up, while two others handcuffed me on my back, making breathing nearly impossible. I closed my eyes and knew that this was going to be the end of my baby's life.

In between crying for insulin and even blacking out a few times, I eventually asked, "So, if my baby dies because you guys refuse me insulin, you will get sued, correct?"

A nurse looked me straight in the eye, speaking in a calm, professional voice that I'm sure she was trained to speak with to all of the mental clients. "No, ma'am, we don't have to give you anything," she said before walking away.

I couldn't believe this was real life. I've always loved and stood up for cops, but this did me in. How could they sit and watch a pregnant woman cry out for help while sipping coffee and laughing like I was just crazy and didn't matter? I know that most police are good people who are looking out for our safety, but in this case, I felt like they didn't understand my needs. I also know that many people are treated much worse than I was, but I'd never been through something like this, and all I wanted to do was go home, fix my sugars, and work on life.

Josh tried telling the police through the door about my diabetes and that this was some kind of mistake, but they had me in custody now, and they were not about to let me go while they were transferring me from the hospital to the mental institution. It was midnight, and as they escorted me to the cop car, I looked over to see my husband in his truck, four hours later, watching his pregnant wife's hands and feet cuffed. Josh was pulling on his hair, trying to figure out a way to save me, but at this moment, I wished I had never even met him. Since I knew he was watching closely, as my hands were facing him, I slipped my ring off and let it hit the ground. I never wanted to see him again.

When I arrived at the institution, the nurses watched my every move. They made me put on a hospital gown, and I almost felt like they were refusing to give me insulin so I would *actually go crazy* and they could keep me longer. They had a teenage boy worker watch me as I slept. I ended up asking him how long he thought I'd be in there, to which he replied, "No one goes home in less than a week." That's when I started really holding my belly and talking to my baby because I knew he wasn't going to make it. I was absolutely humiliated. I knew this kid thought I was nothing more than a nut case, and once he realized who I was he would be telling all of his friends.

I had cried so hard that my eyes were nearly swollen shut, and I was now missing *two* insulin shots and getting sicker by the minute. I kept hoping to wake up from this nightmare soon.

This wasn't the help Josh had expected, and I knew he regretted calling the police. But I didn't care, because, at that moment, I hated Josh with my entire being. Even worse, I was so mad that my mom wasn't fighting to get me out of this situation. Instead, she had encouraged Josh to come and rip my kids from me and knew the cops had taken me in. I think she was just desperate for a change in me. She couldn't watch me battle depression any longer.

Still stuck inside, I grew frantic to get my insulin. If I don't take my shots every three hours, I will get extremely sick and eventually die (which is why the disease is called "DIEabetes"). I can only live for so many days without insulin, and the baby I was carrying could easily die from insulin shock if I didn't get that shot soon. Instead of helping to stabilize my health, the workers in the hospital just kept me in a closed-off room. If I wasn't depressed before, I certainly was now.

Everything was uncomfortable. They took my cell phone, and they wouldn't let me make any calls. I had no way of calling my parents or anyone for help. The hospital was full of teenage workers who didn't seem to know what they were doing. The eighteen-year-old boy who was assigned to sit and watch me also did so when I went to the bathroom and while I showered. Feeling so humiliated, I thought to myself that I would never recover from being sent here. I was sure I was going to be stuck in there for a week or longer, and that my baby was going to die because I had no medication. Now, I really wanted to get out of here and end my life. Without my kids, my freedom, and my family, I had nothing left.

Early the next morning, a therapist came in and sat calmly by my side. Still panicking that my child's life was at major risk, I felt like I really was going crazy. It was everything I had in me not to get up and start throwing punches, but I managed to stay calm by gritting my teeth. I still couldn't believe this was legal.

I was weak, lonely, and felt like I wouldn't ever be able to rise above this mess. I even told them my name was Sarah James because I didn't want the teenagers to recognize me and sell this story to the tabloids. With my luck, I knew the tabloids could really twist this into something even worse than it was, as they are good at doing. I asked the therapist when I could go home, and she calmly replied, "Your husband has been waiting outside and walking circles all night. We are going to allow him to come in and be interviewed to see if you can go home."

"So, have you spoken to my mom?"

"Yes," she said. "She told us you have always been this way and need serious help."

At this moment my head was spinning. My mom said that? The one who has a heart of gold and would do anything for me? I couldn't believe it. Why would she do that to me?

A few minutes later, Josh walked in with my wedding ring, and before he said anything, he put the ring back on my finger right in front of the teenage boy and therapist. He looked at me and said, "This is not what I intended to happen. I'm going to get you in my truck and take you home and fix this. I am so sorry."

I couldn't even look him in the eyes. Had no one been watching, I would have hit him, but I played along because I knew the therapist was watching. She asked him many questions about me, and he lied about everything. He said this was a mistake, and that I'm just a diabetic—not depressed or suicidal. He demanded they let me go or he would get a lawyer involved. She had him sign some papers, and they walked me out to my car.

I was still handcuffed until I reached his vehicle, and I was naked under the hospital gown I was still wearing. The teenage boy, with a face mask and gloves on, carried my clothes and followed us to the car. This only made me feel like a walking disease.

I didn't talk the entire way home, but I was relieved to finally get my insulin shot and some food. Sure, I was thankful that Josh came to save the baby and me, but I still thought it was all his fault. I made him take me to my mom's so I could confront her and take my children from her. I walked in and stared her and my father in the eyes, saying nothing more than, "Fuck you," before grabbing my kids and walking out. I have never spoken to my mom like that. She was my best friend, and I felt betrayed. I couldn't believe that my mom had tried to keep me in there longer by telling the hospital I was depressed and suicidal, not even knowing what was being done to the baby and me.

Right as we got home, Josh told me that things were getting to a point where he just couldn't handle me anymore, so I slid my wedding ring off my finger and handed it to him. He grabbed my hand and put the ring back on my finger while telling me he was going to stay at his mom's house for a while.

I didn't talk to Josh or my mom for about a month, which was nearly the rest of the pregnancy. My doctor started a lawsuit with the institution, but I told him I didn't have the money, time, or mental stability to relive that moment in court, and I let it go. He told me how lucky I was that this baby was alive. I began to have panic attacks so badly after that night that I would black out and fall. I was on bed rest until the end of my pregnancy because just walking to the kitchen would cause me to take a tumble. Josh would often try to check on me, and I'd just force him to leave. I wanted him to feel some type of pain like the pain he had caused me.

Still keeping up with my last few doctor appointments, I went in for a routine ultrasound near my due date. The doctor said that he needed to get the baby out right away, but he didn't say why. In a panic, I started to worry that maybe something had happened to the baby when I was at the mental institution and didn't get my insulin, or afterward, when my body was under so much stress that my blood sugar levels were not leveling out. It's very high risk for a diabetic to even have a baby, and several diabetics I know were never able to have children. What I had been through emotionally and physically just made things more dangerous.

I immediately called Josh's boss, and he told me he would have Josh get to the hospital as quickly as he could. Then, I asked my parents to drive me to the hospital where the doctor would perform the emergency C-section. I walked right in, and there stood ten nurses who sat me down on the bed and moved with great speed to prep me for surgery. Panicking, I screamed at the thought of the epidural needle and asked them to please wait for Josh. They said that it was an emergency, so they couldn't wait, and my mom wrapped her arms tightly around me. My ear was pressed against her chest, and I could hear her heart beating fast. She wanted to take every ounce of anxiety and fear away from me with that hug. It was like the pain of what I had said to her just weeks earlier didn't even matter. As they started to rush me down the hall, Josh finally made it to my side, with pieces of drywall still all over his body. I instantly calmed down once he was by my side.

The doctor came in, and I saw him looking down at me with his head in hands, his face stern and serious. He looked so distraught, and it dawned on me that I might be about to deliver a dead baby. Josh was there, too, and he was focused on the baby and was asking so many questions that the doctor told him he needed to calm down and be strong for me because I was in a state of shock and terror. The last thing I remember is seeing the baby pulled out, but I only heard silence—no crying, no talking. Nothing. Even though it seemed like an eternity, the whole thing was over, and the baby was out in twenty minutes. Broncs Weston McKee was officially here.

I was so drugged and zoning in and out that I don't even remember going back to my room, but I do remember at one point opening my eyes to find my best friend Cayla at the foot of my bed, rubbing my feet. I zoned back out, and when I opened my eyes again, it was just my mom. I smiled and held her hand and asked, "How much does he weigh? Have you held him yet?"

She replied with tears in her eyes, "Sis, they sent us all home. I haven't seen him or Josh since the surgery, but I talked to the doctor and things are not good. Baby Broncs is very sick."

Being so exhausted from the stress of the situation, I must have passed out again, because I woke up much later in the hospital room all alone. I couldn't move, and no one else was there. Even Josh was nowhere to be found, and I called for the nurse to ask where my family and the baby were. She told me to rest and left without responding to the questions I so desperately wanted to be answered. I was paralyzed, as the epidural hadn't worn off, and I must have drifted off to sleep at some point again. Six hours later, the same nurse came in again, and I asked if my child was dead. She responded very flatly that she couldn't answer that.

I couldn't understand what was going on. Josh finally entered my room, but he had no information about what was happening with our baby either. He had tried to follow the nurses back to the NICU (neonatal intensive care unit) room, but they shut the door on him. All he could do was watch through the window as they stuck tubes all over his baby to save his life. I was so out of it and so confused, begging Josh for answers, "Why is no one telling me what's going on? What is happening to my child?" It was seven hours since the baby was born, and we still hadn't been told if he was alive. The baby had been born four weeks early and weighed over ten pounds, but my other two children were born a month early as well. After no explanation from the doctor or the nurse, Josh had had enough and finally erupted and said that they needed to tell us something—anything. He was in full-on Papa Bear mode, and the nurse took him by the arm, and they disappeared again. Once again, I passed out from the stress and medications I was on.

At 3:00 AM, Josh still wasn't back in my room. I didn't know where I was, and I was still so drugged and out of it. The nurse came into my room after I called the front desk and cried for her to please help me find my husband and baby. She quietly came to my room, picked me up, and put me in a wheelchair. She told me she was taking me to see Josh as we approached the door of the NICU. I knew from my previous births that the NICU was for babies who were premature or very ill when they were born and often had to stay there for days, months, or weeks—depending on how fragile their health was. I knew our baby was a healthy weight, even though he was born prematurely, and since neither Gannon nor Jaxie had been in the NICU, I couldn't imagine why he was in there.

I was not prepared for what I saw through the NICU doors. All I could see was Josh standing over a baby whose little body was covered in cords and needles. A bright heat lamp was shining down on him, and Josh was crying and praying while standing over him. We were not allowed to touch him, and he was under a plastic dome. The nurse wheeled my chair next to Josh, where I sat next to him and watched him cry over the baby.

"Mackenzie," he sobbed, "They told me that he has holes in his heart." I had never seen Josh so inconsolable.

I thought it must be my fault that my baby was so sick, and my head felt like a dark tornado was spinning inside of it. How could I have been so careless through this pregnancy to cause so much stress on the baby? I wasn't allowed to touch him for a whole week, but I visited every day. When my milk came in, I rubbed some of it on a cloth so they could place it beside my son in hopes he would know my smell. Was I going to have a sick child forever? I knew it would take some time to know what was ahead for little Broncs.

Thankfully, he got a little bit stronger each passing day. After two weeks of not holding him—it had felt like an eternity—I could finally hold him, and I couldn't wait. Wearing Josh's baggy T-shirt and no bra, I stretched the shirt out and had them tuck the baby under in right against my skin. My entire body melted, and I shook, cried, and smelled the top of his head. Josh was beaming and snapped a photo of the magical moment.

Within a few more days, I was finally able to nurse him for the first time, but he had to stay in the NICU for about four weeks and take heart medication. Josh and I stayed at the Ronald McDonald House near the hospital so we could be close by and see Broncs as much as we could. My parents and my grandpa helped watch the other kids and take Gannon to school while we were there.

I was so thankful for the care that Broncs got at the hospital, and I quickly realized that it was a miracle he had survived. He is my little blessing child, and even though he still gets sick often, I just love to watch him run around while I think about how lucky we are to have him in our lives.

That second month when Broncs finally got to come home, I started developing severe postpartum depression (PPD). I hadn't experienced this after Gannon and Jaxie were born, so I was confused as to why I felt so terrible and that I had no purpose in life. People would tell me that moms should never feel like that and that I should be over the moon to have added another little one to our family. I started to feel like I was being selfish for feeling so sad and hopeless all the time, but I later found out that it's very common for stay-at-home moms to get depressed. Even though we love our children and are so thrilled that they are in our lives, moms still need to socialize with others. I did have a friend who would come over to visit me, and this helped a lot, because I was so jealous that Josh got to go to work and be around people, while I had to stay at home to cook, clean, and look after our kids.

Every day, though, I started feeling worse. Although I was depressed, I didn't have the energy to motivate myself to make a change, and I didn't feel like Josh would understand why I was so down. We were technically husband and wife, but there was little to no intimacy shared between us, which left yet another hole in my life.

I began to have very selfish thoughts. I was only just twenty-one, and my whole life since I was sixteen was spent having kids with the same man. I began wondering if there was something (or someone) better out there, and whether or not Josh and I would even be together if we didn't have kids. I worried that I would never have fun in my young life, and these thoughts ate at me as I began craving more attention. Josh wasn't giving me the same kind of attention he had when we were younger, and I felt he was no longer attracted to me since my struggle with PPD.

I began sneaking behind Josh's back and going to the bars with my friends. Finally, I had something fun in my life, and I started getting attention from other guys while I was out. I met a man, and we started talking frequently. I felt terrible doing this to Josh and knew it was wrong to cheat, but I guess I was so down and out that I thought this was the only thing to give me the boost I needed. One night when I was over at my parents' house with the kids, I got a text from Josh. All it said was, "I know everything. I'm moving out." Someone saw me out with this guy and shared all the dirty details with him. This was just the start of a big downward spiral for me.

I had no way to pay the bills, and I had so little food. All the money I had was spent on food and supplies for the kids, so I wasn't eating much and got so skinny that I looked skeletal. From being so malnourished, my milk dried up, so I couldn't nurse Broncs anymore, but I was too proud to ask my parents or Josh for help. And I had decided it was time to have my tubes tied around this time, which only messed my sugars and hormones up even more.

Josh would try to come back and sometimes would feel so bad for me he would leave groceries on my doorsteps because he saw how skinny I was getting. One day when he was over at my place visiting the kids, we got into an argument. He said that he felt like he was enabling me by just being there and helping me out. He begged me to get help and said that no one knew what to do—even my mom was worried about me. Later that night, I was in the bathtub to relax a little while Josh looked after the kids. After a good soak, I noticed how quiet it had gotten in the house. I wrapped a towel around myself and opened the bathroom door. Josh was gone and so were my kids.

I called Josh's cell, but I got his voicemail. So I left an angry message saying that I was about to call the cops and tell them my children had been kidnapped. When I called the police station, though, the cops told me that since Josh was their father, it couldn't be considered a kidnapping. Jumping in the car, I drove straight to his parents' house, because I knew that's where he would be staying with the kids, but as hard as I banged on the door, no one answered. His truck was there, and all the lights in the house were on, so I knew they had to be inside. It became clear that his parents were helping him hide the kids from me.

Later, I found out that my mom had orchestrated this whole thing with Josh. When I found out the kids were at her house, I called and screamed in a fit of rage. "How dare you take my kids from me?" I was an absolute mess, and instead of having my back, my mom—the person who vowed to always stand by me—went behind my back and made a plan with Josh to protect me from myself. It would take a long time for me to recover and forgive my family, Josh, and his family for this mess that I had actually created. I could forget about straightening my crown at this time because I couldn't even *find* my crown. That's how lost I was.

Things were not getting any better after my kids were taken. It had been days since I'd seen them. It was too dangerous for my mental health to sit alone at my silent house that was usually so loud and full of life. I tried going out with friends and even stayed the night with the same guy I got caught with in hopes of getting my mind off of things. Sitting on my living room floor in the dark, I felt so alone, and I had no idea how I was going to pay my bills and get my kids back. And all of a sudden, a voice inside of me (that I now know was God) told me to get up and look in the mirror. When I did, I saw a Post-it on my mirror that I had placed there long ago. I had forgotten all about it, and I did a double take, moving in closer to read it. What was written on that Post-it was simply: *What is to be is up to me.* That's all.

I told myself in that moment that although I wouldn't be able to predict if Josh would ever take me back or trust me again, I *could* work to get my kids back. I did hear from friends that Josh wasn't doing too well, and out of anger from being separated from me, he was drinking a lot.

Looking back, I wish I had listened to him about getting help sooner, but I also came to understand that as much as someone else might want you to get help, it's only going to make a difference if *you* make the decision to get better for yourself. You can't do it for anyone else. I also chose to just make the decision to become a better person from the inside rather than talk about it. I never called Josh because I just knew God would work everything out for us. I knew Josh and my mom loved me, and had they kept babying me, I might not have ever gotten better. I couldn't see how bad I truly was in the moment, but making better choices and taking care of myself would speak volumes. I hoped that would bring my two best friends back—my mom and my husband. I wasn't in this rut because of anyone but myself, and if I wanted my life to improve, it was going to be up to me and only me. I couldn't rely on anyone else—not Josh, my mom, my kids, or this other guy I'd been seeing—to give my life joy and meaning. My happiness and success were up to me.

Crowning Achievement:

When I say I am a follower of Christ, I do not mean I think I am perfect. I mean that I am too weak to handle life on my own. I am learning in life to turn to God when I hit rock bottom because some things are too hard for us to bear alone. When I finally let it all go and gave my life to him, I started to see the light at the end of the tunnel, but it took opening my eyes and being willing to make that change.

Chapter 20

WHAT IS TO BE IS UP TO ME

In repentance and rest is your salvation, in
quietness and trust is your strength.
Isaiah 30:15

Seeing that Post-it was like a slap in the face from God to get my life back together, but I had no idea how I'd do it. Sure, I'd tried many things in the past to make a living. During my senior year in high school, my mom took me to Best Buy, and I bought a $900 camera. I wanted to be a photographer, but I quickly realized that I liked being in *front* of the camera more than being *behind* it. I also got my cosmetology license and gave working in a salon a try, but that wasn't for me, either. In the back of my mind, though, I had always thought of trying something with fitness, so maybe this was my time to give it a shot.

I have such a love for fitness because my mom was very graceful in the way she taught us to be healthy. She didn't shove it down our throats that we had to eat "this" and "that." She didn't make us work out all the time, but she simply set a good example for us. We watched her eat healthy food and get up and run each morning. The whole town knew her for her running, and one time I actually made her a shirt that said, "I Run This Town," because Miami is so small that she could run ten miles and make a loop around the whole town every day.

I always wanted to be like her—all of my siblings did, too, but we all had our own talents. I had been successful early on with gymnastics and competitive cheer. My sister Kaylee is an animal in the gym and can lift like crazy. Zeke is a fitness coach, and he's so strong that people call him "Zeke the Freak." My oldest sister, Whitney, runs marathons, so being healthy is a way of life for all of us.

I thought that I could also incorporate all I had learned about health from having diabetes. Although I struggle daily with this disease, I've become so educated because of it, and I have God to thank for showing me the way to better health. I can now look at a plate of food and calculate carbs, fats, and proteins into insulin. I realized I could use my knowledge to help people because of my disease, and I knew that taking something so awful and turning it into something good would give me satisfaction. Plus, with all my training for fitness competitions and the connections I had made, why not start a fitness program? I sat down and looked at what was in front of me. I had no money, but I did have that nice camera and a laptop I had bought myself from selling crocheted items.

"What is to be is up to me." I kept repeating it to myself when a light bulb went off in my head. I was going to use my

knowledge and love for fitness to create a workout program. My sister had her own backyard gym, and she agreed to let me film there. I thought long and hard about a name and came up with BodyByMac. It stuck. When I told my family and friends about my idea, some of them laughed. One family member even asked me if I really thought anyone would buy my workout program.

That was discouraging, but my mom had always let me do my thing. She would watch people look at me and doubt me, and she would always say, "I'm going to sit back and watch, because Mackenzie blows my mind every time." It was an awkward time between the two of us, because she was the one who told Josh that he needed to take the kids away from me, and I was still angry at her. But she was right, and sometimes the truth hurts.

No one believed in me, but I couldn't control what others thought. I could only control the outcome for myself. I started carefully designing the program, recording, and saving up to start a website. I didn't even have enough money to buy food for myself, and I remember that if I was visiting people, I would go into their kitchens and grab a banana just so I could have fuel for the day. This is when most people give up, and everyone kept telling me to just go work in a salon because I was so broke. I started to think that maybe they were right, so I applied to one, was hired on the spot, and then I decided not to even show up the next day. That night I realized that I couldn't work there and focus on creating my own fitness business at the same time. I just had a bigger picture in my head. I would just have to be my same stubborn self and tune everyone else out.

One night around this time, Josh let himself into the house at 3:00 AM with the key he still had. He told me he knew what I'd been doing with friends and another male I had been talking to, because people were talking, and he told me he was ashamed.

I wondered how in the heck I'd even gotten to this point where I felt so low.

I explained to Josh that I knew I had made mistakes and I was sorry. Begging him to understand what I had been going through, I promised to fix those issues deep inside of me that caused me to cheat. I was so lucky that Josh was willing to step away and give me space and freedom during that time, even if it made me hit rock bottom. I had read a great book that taught me something important—something I could apply to my own life. It said that "hurting people hurt other people." That was so true in my case. I was hurting deep down about my childhood, struggling in school, having diabetes, and being a mom before I could really become something myself. As a result, I hurt Josh because I had no way of healing my inner pain. Josh showed me during all this that he believed in me and was willing to give me a second, third, and fourth chance if needed. I had told him I was going to be fine, and I started looking for ways to bounce back and get out of this dark cloud I had been under.

He slowly walked toward me, and as soon as my head hit that sweet spot in his chest, I melted as he wrapped his arms around me. I felt warmth as the pain and anxiety rushed out of my body. Josh's and my mother's hugs are magical and melt me every time. I began to sob because I missed his warmth so much. A few days later, Josh came back home for good with the kids.

Things started settling back into place for us, and things were looking up. I knew tax season was here. When our $4,000 refund check arrived, Josh knew I was behind on rent and bills. I needed groceries, and we were living on a budget, but one thing we all knew is that I will do what I want, and no one can stop me.

Thankfully, Josh has never been controlling when it comes to my decisions or how I spend money. I know a lot of husbands would have stopped their wives from gambling that money on a business and made them catch up on bills or share it, but Josh gave me free rein to use our tax refund for my business. Everyone around me thought I was absolutely nuts, but Josh let me do my thing. Had Josh told me no, I could possibly still be working in a salon with no business of my own. I used every penny of the refund and scraped up more to create and trademark my website for BodyByMac so I could own it for life.

It took six long, exhausting months, but I created my own four-week fitness program. To make money to survive, I would crochet head warmers on the side and sell them, and when I say "survive," I mean about $500 a month. My family still didn't see things quite the way I did, though. They didn't understand how I could risk so much money to possibly make nothing in return. In my mind, it was a jump to take $4,000 and turn it into $4,000,000. My mom, familiar with my incredible work ethic since I was a child, was always impressed with my ability to stretch a dime, and never being a big spender, she would just smile at me and say, "Don't let the world stop you."

When I finally launched my website and workouts, I made $20,000 the first week! I watched my phone light up, and it was exciting to see how my fans believed in me. Even though people in my hometown were already annoyed that I got on TV for getting pregnant at sixteen, now I felt I was doing something to be proud of. Many people probably expected me to fail (maybe even hoped I would), but now, I go to Walmart, and people will call me "BodyByMac" and ask me for advice. No one is questioning or laughing at me now, but it took me four rough years to get here. People start businesses all the time that they get excited about, but many of them fail. Because I was consistent and didn't give up, I turned my dream into reality.

The first thing I did when I got paid was to go grocery shopping, and I didn't even have to look at my bank account first! Next, I paid off my car loan. I've become really good at staying out of debt, and I try to pay for everything up front in cash. In the beginning, I wanted to buy all the materialistic things because I never had seen that much money, but now I've let go of that. Now, I strive to be more giving. Any time there is a chance to give, donate, or help, I try to put my own wants aside and give to others. Life is so short and I'd rather bless people than take my money to the grave with me. I watched my mom do that no matter how broke she was, and I appreciate that now I can give more and help others. Recently, I was so happy to be able to give to an organization for homeless vets. It was an amount that would have made me sick to my stomach to part with in my earlier days, so I love that I can afford to give more now.

My family didn't tell me until recently that they thought I was doing well. Sometimes I worry that they are annoyed with me because they went to college and did everything right. They must look at me sometimes and think, *"What the heck?"* I get that vibe, but at the same time, I know they love me and are happy that I finally found my calling.

It does upset me when people say that BodyByMac is only successful because I was on TV. I had to crawl out of a very dark spot to get here. I did this when I didn't have many followers. MTV had dropped me—I wasn't on TV anymore. I didn't even have money for groceries, but I built this from the ground up. I promise I would have become something without MTV. There are a lot of people out there who became successful without reality TV, so when someone thinks I'm incapable of success on my own, they have no clue what I went through to get here. I took every opportunity that was thrown my way and ran with it.

I'm definitely more proud of my business than any other thing I've done. After two years, people started reaching out to me and wanting to collaborate with me or take me under their wings to make my business bigger. I had to turn a lot of people down, which is a good problem to have, but it just shows me that people do see something in me. When people talk about TV, I say, "Yeah, I got pregnant at sixteen. That was handed to me." But this is my baby that I rock. It's my pride and joy. I get to wake up every day and work the job that makes me happy. I feel so blessed, and had I not hit rock bottom, BodyByMac might not exist.

Crowning Achievement:

Life was rough and pushed me to seek God for help. I felt like I had nothing, but I had something very powerful. I had a choice. A choice to dig deep, look at what I had, and get a little uncomfortable by taking chances. Things started getting better from the inside when I turned to God for strength and had faith in his guidance. I crawled out of a dark place and now get to spend every day doing what I love.

Chapter 21

SOMETHING SEEMS OFF

Yet you do not know what tomorrow will bring. What is your life?
For you are a mist that appears for a little time and then vanishes.
James 4:14

After this incredible rough patch dealing with postpartum depression, breaking up and making up with Josh, and starting my business, things were finally looking up. We moved into a bigger home, and I was really happy with where my marriage was. My family and I hadn't been on TV in years, and my mom agreed to make a workout program with me for BodyByMac. I thought it would be so fun, so we got on our workout gear and went to the gym to film.

As I've mentioned before, my mom had been so fit and healthy for as long as I could remember, but this day, after only a little physical activity, my mom was out of air. I was worried, but she was dismissive, telling me she thought it was probably just a symptom of menopause, and laughed. She was now forty-eight years old, and she said that was just something to be expected as women age. A few days went by, though, and she wasn't feeling much better, so she scheduled a doctor's appointment, where she was told she had bronchitis and was given an inhaler. Still, she insisted on filming the rest of the workout tape with me, but I noticed when she came to pick me up the day we were going to film, she had Band-Aids all over her arms. I saw blood dripping and scrapes all over her body. I was so startled that I yelled, "Oh my gosh, Mom! What in the world?" She laughed and said that she blacked out while running and took a tumble on the pavement. I was worried and told her we didn't have to film. She just laughed about it and said she had hoped no one saw her fall.

Something seemed off with her, but she wanted to finish filming, so we did. I could tell she was powering through the workouts because the woman is tough as nails, but when I went home to edit the tapes, I couldn't even use some of the footage because her breathing was so loud. I didn't want to say anything, though, and embarrass her.

A few days later, my mom went back to her local doctor and they caught something on her X-ray that worried them. They were so worried, in fact, that they told her to get to Joplin, Missouri, immediately, where there was a bigger hospital.

My dad drove my mom to the ER and ended up waiting for over two hours. The whole time they were at the hospital, my mom was texting us about someone coming to the ER for a small rash and how funny she thought that was along with all the other hilarious ER stories.

After a long wait, my mom was called back to the exam room and told that they would need to do some scans. When finished with the scans and tests, the doctor handed her a paper explaining what was wrong with her. He said that she had a tumor in her lungs the size of a grapefruit and that it was wrapped around her windpipe. He was shocked that she could even breathe—that's how bad it was.

When my mom broke the news to the rest of the family and me, the word "cancer" didn't scare me much. It barely registered with me. I thought, "A lot of people have cancer and beat it, and besides, it's just a tumor. They can take out tumors!" But my mom went on to explain that the doctor said she didn't just have one tumor—he said there were also tumors in her brain. It felt like I'd been stabbed in the heart when she told us that she had so many tumors in her brain that doctors stopped counting them on one side at forty. This was so confusing to me. That very day, she had been jumping around and working out with me. She had lifted a fifty-pound weight over her head one hundred times with my sister Kaylee the night before. She had been running laps around me. I refused to believe that cancer could keep her down. She couldn't be *that* sick.

After we got the news, Josh drove me over to my sister Whitney's house. I was hysterically screaming, crying, and blacking out, and my sister tried her best to calm me down. She and I have a special bond, and she has such a motherly instinct to her that sometimes she feels like another parent to me. I collapsed into Whitney's arms, and she just held me and let me cry while she tried to remain strong for me. Eventually, the sadness became too much, though, and she broke down with me, and we cried and cried and cried. Our mom—the woman who always made things better—was sick. The woman who had all the tools and resources that you could think of, and if someone said no to her, she would find a way to make it happen. How in the world did she get cancer? Why would God let this happen to someone who had so much love and grace to give?

The next morning, all four of her kids headed to the hospital to be with her. We walked in, and my dad was by her side with no color to his skin. He looked lifeless, didn't speak to any of us, and just stared off into space. We were still confused as to the seriousness of her condition. When we tried to hug our dad, he just sat there. The woman who had brought him to God, the one he had been in love with since he was a kid, was now sick. The woman we called the "Energizer Bunny" and our everything—how could this be?

Maybe it would be as simple as surgery and some chemo to live another fifty years or more. When the doctor came in, we anxiously waited. He looked at all of us and said, "I'm so sorry. Your mother has stage four lung cancer, and it has started to metastasize to other parts of her body."

Silence filled the room as we all became numb. It was a nightmare we were all waiting to wake up from. I vividly remember pinching my skin as hard as I could and being so disappointed when I felt the pain, because that meant that I wasn't dreaming and that this was real. Us kids sobbed and sobbed. Then I looked over in the corner of the room, and there stood my mom's parents and sister. They looked so weak, like they just wanted to touch and heal her, but we all knew this was all out of our control. My mom had spent her whole life fixing our problems, and now there was nothing we could do to help her. During all this sorrow and uncertainty, I never saw fear in my mom's face or tears in her eyes. We knew she was a warrior who could overcome anything. We all believed that to our cores.

As the days went by, we learned more about the type of cancer my mom had. We knew there were stages of cancer, and she had advanced stage 4 cancer. You hear of people beating cancer all the time, so we held strongly on to hope. The doctor, however, always had an odd look on his face when we spoke hopefully. He finally told us words that stung the most. He said, "This cancer is incurable, and she has three to eight months to live." There was never talk of her possibly beating this horrible disease with the right treatment.

Again, my mom showed her incredible strength when she told the family that while the doctor can tell her how long she might have left, God would be the one who determined her last day on Earth. She may only have months or a few years, but he wanted us all to remember that she was willing to give this disease all the fight and strength that she could.

After what seemed like hours of everyone holding one another sobbing, my mom calmly stood up and told us that she wanted to go to the hospital chapel, and as she started to walk toward it, we all silently followed her. She stepped up to the pulpit to pray, and this was the only time I ever saw her cry about her cancer, unless she cried behind closed doors where none of us could see. I thought for sure that standing here, she would ask God why he gave her cancer, but she didn't. Instead, she asked God for forgiveness for any wrongdoing she had done in life and for the will to fight this disease. It was the most selfless prayer I had ever heard.

"Oh my gosh, God. I'm *so sorry* I took my life for granted. Please forgive me for anyone I've ever gossiped about or anything bad I have done." It was a heartbreaking moment listening to her personal conversation with God as she came to terms that she was going to have quite a struggle ahead of her. When she got back to her room, she looked up at all of us and said, "Always be kind, guys." She wasn't scared to die. She was scared of wasting any more time on Earth not honoring God and being kind to others. That phrase of "always be kind" began to spread like wildfire and became her motto. That first hospital stay was a long week. By the end of it, none of us had any tears left. My dad was barely a functioning human and couldn't leave her side.

The day she arrived home, news of her diagnosis had traveled fast on social media and by word of mouth, and the whole town was coming together to help her fight. Our church called a prayer meeting for that evening. There were no parking spots left, and the pews were packed. When you spend your life helping others like my mom did, the person you are will come back to you. That is what life is truly about. All these people were crying so loudly for my mom that you couldn't even hear the praying. People stood up and spoke, and then my mom got up as we all held our breath and prayed. She made a point of telling people that they mattered and that they shouldn't waste their lives. "You must know you're important and how loved you are," she said to them. She always had a way of making things about other people and not herself, and this was a perfect example.

Another church called about a worship night weeks later, and she was only getting sicker. We pulled up, and she was breathing heavily. We told her she didn't need to be there, that prayer night could still go on, but she insisted my dad help her to the front door. She went up at the end of the service and made a beautiful and, yet again, selfless speech letting everyone know just how much God loves them. She begged them to stop wasting time doing anything other than loving others.

Later that night when my family was back at her house, she told us that she had heard God's voice during radiation telling her that she was meant to be a speaker long ago, but she was too busy at the time. Now, she said, it was her time to share the word of God, and that he had told her it's your breath and my lungs that will help you. She gave a powerful speech about living life again, and we had a feeling this was just the beginning of something bigger. And it was.

Life began to change rapidly, and she wasn't wasting a single second. She had quite a social media following from stealing people's hearts on *Teen Mom*, and the day she was diagnosed, January 2, 2017, she made a single post about her illness that went viral. The next day and the day after that, she woke up and did the same thing. She began waking up at 3:00 AM every morning to spend time with God before writing whatever was in her heart. People from all over would anxiously wait for her powerful positive message of the day.

Before we knew it, people were calling from all over the country to have her speak, and her schedule was booked. She decided not to go back to work that following semester, and she started chemo and lost so much weight, along with all the hair on her head and body. When she first walked into the house after shaving her head, it was an emotional moment, but my dad acted like his eyes just saw an angel from Heaven. He walked across the room to hug his beautiful wife.

She was getting sicker and weaker, but somehow, she was able to get up on stage and give the most inspirational speeches wherever she went. Some churches would give her a "love donation," which she put toward their house so my dad wouldn't have debt when she was gone. Even during times when most people would put their needs first, she was still putting the needs of others before hers. Even though she had dozens of tumors taking over her brain, my mom was determined to spread God's word and love until the day she died.

MTV took notice of her story since people were talking about it all over the internet, and when they asked her if they could film a special about her story, she replied, "If I can talk about my love for God, then YES!" MTV truly loved my mom. One time, years before, there was a reunion in New York the same weekend as the New York Marathon. But there was a hurricane that year, and even though people from all over the world had flown in, they canceled the race at the last minute. Running the New York Marathon had been my mom's dream. It's a very expensive and hard race to get into. A lady on the elevator who had traveled all the way from another country to participate had told my mom that people were going to get up and run it anyway. I could see the wheels in her head spinning. And I was right. She got up that morning and went and ran the full marathon in Central Park. No training, no prepping. She just got up and ran and then had to film a full day with Dr. Drew. It was always a joke MTV would tell. That she got up and ran a marathon no problem before the reunion. It was such a happy moment in life for her. She may not have run the real race. But she ran in the exact place with the real runners.

Weeks went by, and I was scheduled to fly to New York City for a photoshoot and a talk show appearance. I had planned to take Josh with me. I was sitting in my mom's backyard with her and my sister, and I simply said, "Guess what? I get to go to New York over the weekend!"

I hadn't asked my mom to be my "plus one," because I honestly didn't want her to have to pass it up because of how sick she was, so Josh and I had already begun to pack our bags. Her eyes got so big when I told her, as she had apparently just been thinking about how she wanted to visit Central Park one more time. She looked at Josh and said, "Sorry, kid. I'm hopping on that plane."

I turned and looked at Josh while laughing, and he simply winked at me and whispered in my ear, "I got the kids. Let her go." I was so thankful for Josh for letting her go in his place, and she was ecstatic to join me. I really cherish those trips. Even though her doctors advised her not to fly because she was so ill, she went anyway. She trusted God, and said, *"I'm LIVING— not DYING!"*

When we arrived at the Viacom studio, I told her to stick by my side. She was so skinny—like skin and bones. The studio had no idea my mom was coming, but everyone laughed and fell in love with her when she walked into the salon and said, "Who wants to do my hair?" She was bald! The producer deemed her the "Monday Mom" on the show, and she got to go sit with the crowd in the audience. It was a highly viewed episode, and it was totally unplanned. It was just incredible watching the people near her who wanted to touch and hug her.

Later, we went back to my hotel room, and a tabloid company came to do a podcast with me. My mom sat to the side and watched me having trouble with the interview. The tabloid podcast host was trying to get some gossip out of me, asking me if I thought one of the other Teen Moms was pregnant, since she was looking bloated. Sensing my discomfort, my mom jumped in, took over, and started talking about body shaming. The podcast host shied away from any more gossipy questions, as my mom schooled him on body positivity.

I always wanted to be someone who inspired others, but it was really my mom who people adored. She had a way of shining, and I am certain that God used me to make sure she could share her love with millions of people. She was a Christian who stepped out of that comfort zone of only belonging with other Christians. She is the one who taught me that the best relationship with God is a personal one.

One doctor who was helping her once said to my family that he'd been my mom's doctor for two years, and that she had reached more people than any preacher he had ever known—even those who had preached for more than fifty years. She took every opportunity, was open-minded, and accepted everyone. If more people were like her, more people would feel welcome to go to church. To this day, I get hundreds of messages in my inbox telling me that she changed peoples' lives.

One day around this time, she and I were able to sit down and talk openly about the mental institution. She apologized for thinking I was getting the proper help I needed and not knowing how I was really treated. She explained that it broke her every day to see me struggle with mental health, and the more she tried to help, the worse I got, which was true. To this day, I still live with the pain of the words I said to her the day I came home from the hospital. She had forgiven me before I even left her house that day, but I needed her to know what a special human she was to me and many others.

We all knew that my mom had a long road ahead of her, but people got cancer all the time and survived, and she was going to do all it took to live. Her family, friends, and whole town were ready to fight right beside her, because if there was anything we knew, it was that Angie Douthit was a warrior, and since she called me a "warrior" and an "overcomer" many times, too, I was happy to remind her that I learned from her example.

Crowning Achievement:

Life is fragile. My mother—a God-fearing, healthy-eating, marathon-running fitness lover—ended up with stage 4 lung cancer, but she told me that it is *not about the days God gives us on this Earth, but what we do with the days he gives us.* I am guilty of wasting days in nothing but pity, and I can only imagine how this makes Him feel as my Creator. We are not promised a single second, so the worst thing we can do is continue to waste our time on Earth.

Chapter 22

GOING THROUGH THE MOTIONS

Love is patient and kind. Love is not jealous or boastful or proud or rude. It does not demand its own way. It is not irritable, and it keeps no record of being wronged. It does not rejoice about injustice but rejoices whenever the truth wins out. Love never gives up, never loses faith, is always hopeful, and endures through every circumstance.
1 Corinthians 13:4–7

When my mom got sick, my relationship with Josh started to suffer in silence. We were under the same roof, playing the roles of mom and dad, but we were disconnected, both physically and emotionally. Josh worked long hours and would come home, sleep, and repeat. Any time he would try to be intimate, I would shut him down. It got to the point of no touching at all, and I knew eventually he would need someone else to be intimate with. He would beg me, but I just didn't want to be near him. I resented him and started to rethink my life, coming to the awkward headspace of imagining a better life with someone else. I knew if I met someone better, I'd simply leave Josh and move on. I fell in love with him for his quietness and sweet Southern charm, but reading comments on the internet of people questioning how someone fun like me could be with someone as boring as Josh made me want to experiment with someone more fun and outgoing.

I was taking a lot of trips with my mom to her speaking engagements or working on projects with my business during this time, so that became my life. And although I learned my lesson of letting no one run my name into the ground for fast fame, my desire to be back in the spotlight was a huge turnoff for Josh.

Josh was away on the rodeo circuit a good deal of the time, and I actually kind of enjoyed it. I think he did, too, because he was finally getting out and seeing the world. We didn't really check in on one another, either, while he was away, and in retrospect, that was a mistake on both of our parts. While we were so physically and emotionally distant from one another, Josh started falling into the wrong crowd, and I would eventually find out all about what he had been out doing, but not directly from him. Nope. I had to learn through the tabloids that he'd gotten himself into trouble. And when it comes to the tabloids, you never know how far they've stretched the truth.

On the road, Josh and some of his cowboy rodeo friends were inappropriate with a group of women. Now he was back home with me, and I wanted to confront him, but before I did, I wanted to get all the facts.

I found out who this woman was, because I wanted to talk to her and get her version of what happened, and she was insistent that she didn't touch my "ugly husband," as she called him, and that I had the wrong woman. She also blamed me for making things up in my head. Not getting any clarity from her, I called one of the guys whom Josh had been traveling with and put him on speakerphone since Josh was there to listen too. I knew this guy would probably rat on Josh if he'd done something, because I also was aware that he liked me. And guess what? He did just that. I just let him tell the story on speaker, and I'll never forget the look of pain on Josh's face as he heard it.

All the pain of this boiled inside me. I looked at him and had one just thing to say: *"I thought you were my best friend."* At this point, nothing in me wanted to live. Here I was, dealing with the possibility of losing my mom to cancer, and now I had to deal with the truth that Josh was stepping out. He explained it was nothing more than a drunk night and begged me to explain to him why I was no longer intimate with him. If I'm being honest, it wasn't a matter of *if* this was going to happen but *when*. I instantly regretted all the times I begged him to just go have a good night with some whore and get it out of his system because I had no desire to be with him anymore. And finding out from the tabloids instead of him was the worst blow. This is definitely one of those instances where if I weren't on TV, I probably never would have found out. I'm starting to learn that a lot of marriages have secrets that are taken to the grave, and I honestly wish I had never found out. Josh never talked to this woman after that, and she lived several states away, so why did I even have to know?

Although Josh's infidelity was humiliating, it created a breakthrough for me. I thought maybe this was my chance to divorce him and escape, especially since he seemed to be at the same low point that I was in our relationship. I'd done my fair share of cheating and was fantasizing about a relationship with a new man. Maybe we would both be happier with someone else. It was time that we had some brutally honest conversations about where this marriage was going.

I was calm for a few hours. Josh began to realize the rodeo life was no longer for him, and never spoke again to that friend who confirmed to me what happened. We agreed to go to counseling together, and we were actually able to make some breakthroughs. This awful incident opened up several doors for us both to come clean. I told him about how sometimes I had stepped out on him while on vacation with friends, confessing most of the secrets I had ever hidden from him. I told him what had happened to me with those boys when I was younger, and with tears in his eyes, he told me things he'd never been able to talk about too. It felt so good to come clean, as I realized how horrible it feels to keep secrets. He insisted there was nothing more to the situation with that woman. And although my gut still feels there was, it doesn't matter at this point. The moral of my story, I learned, was that we had gotten married way too young and that this marriage had been a hot mess since day one.

When we got home after that first night of counseling, I broke. The pain and anger I held in all came out, and I went through our house with a hammer and shattered every photo of him, the kids, and me together. To this day, I still can't hang pictures of our family in the house. Before all this, the whole house was made up of our beautiful love story, and I realized that the story I had been telling myself wasn't even close to being true. I no longer wanted this kind of life with him. He watched as I packed every belonging he owned and placed it all in the back of his truck. Hoping to never see him again, I selfishly wished he would just disappear so I wouldn't have to share the kids with him.

Still acting out of rage and hurt, I called up my ex—yes, the same ex whom I had always turned to in these situations that seemed to just keep happening between Josh and me. I could always depend on him to pick me up in a low moment, and Josh knew all about it and couldn't stop me. I even took photos with this guy and sent them to Josh. Of course, that didn't help on any front.

Two days later, I had divorce papers ready to go, but Josh wouldn't sign them. He begged me to think about this before making a decision that would change all of our lives. I left and dealt with things the only way I could think of: out of desperation. I was getting plastered by washing down six Benadryl with vodka in hopes that I could block this all out.

Josh, on the other hand, went to my mom's house and told her everything. Although she was disappointed in him (who wouldn't be?), she asked him to forgive me. When he wouldn't talk to me, I told him I'd be back again with the divorce papers in a few days. He ended up moving into his parents' house.

Before I was able to return with the papers, I started getting presents on my doorstep, and I knew they had to be from Josh. Every day for ten days, a gift would appear, and on the eleventh day, there were directions for a detailed scavenger hunt. At the end of the hunt, Josh was waiting for me with a new engagement ring, and he proposed all over again. I found out that even my sister and mom had gotten involved to help plan this. We had recently started filming at this time for *Teen Mom OG,* and they filmed the whole thing. Instead of Josh getting to redeem himself, fans who saw the show complained that MTV must have set the whole thing up, but they didn't. It was all Josh.

When he was changing and wanting me back, he kept telling me over and over how sorry he was. He had even been sending my mom texts that she would then forward to me about how regretful he was. My family couldn't understand why I didn't forgive Josh. My mom told me that I needed to let him in and not give up. Even after all this, she still loved Josh.

He started taking me on romantic, extravagant dates with roses and fancy dinners. It was like we were starting over, except we'd never really gotten to do these things before in our earlier days. I thought we just might have a chance of making our relationship work again, but in the back of my mind, I knew this was all out there for the world to see, and I only looked weak for being with him. I had promised myself my entire life that I would never be a woman who would take back an unfaithful man. How could I dare show everyone who was watching me that I'm actually weak and have such low self-esteem that I couldn't reject his gifts and apologies?

Crowning Achievement:

Sometimes we are so focused on how others did us wrong and our own pain, or even our humiliation about what the world sees of us, that we forget to dig deep and understand how we may have hurt others. This was the first year of my life where I was able to look at all my mistakes and see how wrong they were. I felt the pain of what Josh did to me, so I was able to then understand the pain of the things I had once done to him. And although I hate what Josh has done to me, it is what has helped me be more cautious of the pain I could possibly be causing others. I've also been able to help others who have gone through similar marital experiences. No woman or man should ever let anyone walk all over them. But sometimes we need to love ourselves and recognize the love and forgiveness God has given us that we never deserved. Josh's easy forgiveness of me throughout the years was highly undeserving, and although this has been rough for me, he has taught me how to be more forgiving.

Chapter 23

SHARING MY SECRET

*Be kind to one another, tenderhearted, forgiving
one another, as God in Christ forgave you.*
Ephesians 4:32

As the days wore on after my mom's cancer diagnosis, we still had a hard time believing how sick she was. When we were kids, if we fell, she would tell us, "Get up—you're not dying!" If our legs weren't hanging off, we were fine. She'd just joke that we should rub some dirt on our scratches and wipe ourselves off. She was hardcore and tough. How could she have gotten this terrible disease? Could she have caught this earlier?

Of course, we were hoping for the best, and since she was so young and strong, we were confident she could beat this. But as time went by, I kept worrying that I could lose her someday without telling her about what happened to me as a young child. I planned to tell her, but it never seemed like the "right time." Her health had been suffering more, but every time the doctor gave her three months to live, she surpassed that by living another year. I didn't want to burden her with guilt, but I also wanted to tell her in hopes of healing—she was my best friend and confidante. If I couldn't tell her, who could I tell? But I also knew this could cause a rift in our relationship because she would want to know all the details of when, where, and with whom it happened. Sometimes you hear people saying little girls make stuff up, but I wanted to confront this head-on. I had kept this secret inside for twenty years, and before telling my mom, I wanted to talk to Josh and get some support that I was doing the right thing in telling her. We had been married for ten years at this point when I finally broke down and shared it with him. When I finally got up the nerve to tell him, he was incredibly supportive, and he encouraged me to talk about it with my family.

"You've got to tell your mom," he said, and I knew he was right. However, I didn't want my mom to feel guilty about it. I knew she would. I knew she would blame herself for what happened—for somehow not having the ability to be everywhere at all times to protect me from harm. How could I tell her and reassure her that I didn't hold her responsible for what happened? That I had no resentment toward her and that I just wanted to move on?

I knew it would be difficult to tell her, even though I felt so much relief after just sharing my secret with Josh. Realizing that there would probably never be a right time to tell her, I just decided one day that it was time. I was over at her house, and she was sitting in a chair on her front porch. She looked so small and frail from the cancer ravaging her body, but this might be one of my last chances to share this with her, as we never knew how many days she had left. I finally struck up the nerve and told her I needed to get something off my chest.

After I told her, she just stared straight ahead for a few moments, silent. Was she angry at me for not telling her sooner? Did she think I was making this up? She closed her eyes and pursed her lips. Then, as she slowly began nodding her head she said, "This makes a lot of sense, Mackenzie. This makes a lot of sense."

We went on to discuss how my innocence was robbed, and I told her that losing virginity at such a young age didn't seem like that big of a deal, because I already felt ruined even though it could have been much worse. She told me that whatever I felt, she never wanted me to think that this was something I deserved. This was something evil that someone else had done to me, and it wasn't a punishment for something I had done wrong. While she couldn't take away the experiences, this talk went an incredibly long way in helping me accept myself for who I am and learn that God and parents have unconditional love for their children.

I refused to let her know who did this to me because that wasn't what mattered to me, and she apologized for the time she said I wasn't her baby girl anymore after finding out I had lost my virginity. I know that day was rough on her because she texted me that night that she was the worst mother on this Earth and that she couldn't believe she didn't know. She couldn't stop blaming herself and apologizing, but I kept assuring her that she did nothing wrong and that I had forgiven the men in my heart.

The saddest thing is this happens every day to little girls *and* boys. It has forced me to make decisions with my own children that I wouldn't have thought about before, and I'm very cautious. When we think of abuse, we often envision kids getting kidnapped by strangers and bad things happening, but most of the time, it's right under our roofs with someone we thought we could trust.

All I can say about this chapter of my life is that I'm relieved to have shared what I kept stuffed down inside of me for so long. The shame and sadness I had felt over the years wasn't the result of some horrible things I did, and no matter what, I was still lovable and important. Just as I didn't let getting pregnant as a teen define me, I didn't have to let this abuse define me or hold me back any longer.

Crowning Achievement:

I had to dig deep later in life and turn to God for ways to deal with this. It is His job to deal with me and my sins, and I needed to look to Him for guidance. I have no resentment in my heart because I know these boys were young. I just hope that no child ever has to carry this kind of secret through life. With daily work, I'm learning to focus on fixing myself and being kind and tenderhearted to others, as Christ is with us. Doing this has given me peace and less stress to carry.

Chapter 24

CROSSING THE FINISH LINE

*I have fought the good fight, I have finished
the race, I have kept the faith*
2 Timothy 4:7

t was Thanksgiving, and my dad told us that my mom was really starting to not feel well. I had asked her to speak to the cheer squad I was coaching at the time, and I knew it was getting bad when she said, "Sis, I just want to rest." She continued with her daily posts, but she started to turn down speaking opportunities.

Every year, my sisters and I ran a local 5K around Thanksgiving with our mom to raise money for diabetes. She won it in her age division every year except for the one time she got second place to a lady she had always beaten before. When that happened, she turned to my sister and me and said, "Dang, menopause is slowing me down!" That was only two months before her diagnosis.

This year, I knew she was way too sick to run, so I decided to skip it…or so I thought. At 7:00 AM the morning of the race, I woke up to a text saying, "Get your butt up! I'm not freezing in this race alone." I couldn't believe it. She was actually crazy enough to think she could run this race. I looked out my window, and sure enough, she was in my driveway, ready to pick me up, and no matter how tired I was, it wasn't an option for me to let her run alone.

My sister Whitney had just had a baby via C-section, but she showed up to run as well. Standing near the finish line, we saw Whitney at the front, ready to take off and run as fast as she could. I looked at my mom and said, "Run when you want, walk when you want, but I am not leaving your side." She told me I could run if I wanted, but there was no way I was going to do that. I said, "Mom, if I have to carry you to the end, I will."

She replied, "Oh, I'm going to finish this race, Sis!" Running was so important to her. We knew every runner there because it was a hometown event, and I think a lot of them were nervous for her, but we all knew you couldn't stop her.

The gun went off. We began at a slow jog and walked when we needed to. I kept a close eye on her to make sure we were not overdoing it. We had recently found out that my mom's liver was giving out, and she was very sick. We made it two miles, and I kept telling her, "You got this!"

With just one mile left, she suddenly stopped and let everyone pass. "Mackenzie, this isn't good. Please find me a bathroom."

I sprinted and started knocking on doors of nearby homes with no luck. Her eyes filled with tears as she sat on the ground and calmly said, "It happened." She had messed her pants.

I begged her to just get on my back. I didn't care at all, and I was going to carry her to the finish line. She said, "Please, just help me get home so I can change."

I called my dad, and we had to talk her into getting in the car. She was so embarrassed he had to see his wife like this. She begged me to go on and finish, so I sprinted that last mile alone and cried so loud that I knew neighbors were staring out their windows. I finished and grabbed Whitney, who held me through my tears. She read her texts, grabbed my hand, and said, "Mackenzie, she went home and changed and had someone drop her off at the same spot where she left off so she can finish the race."

We sprinted to meet her and saw how weak she was, but I looked over at Whitney, who had the biggest smile on her face. Running with my mom was her "thing," and she was so proud of her. We each took one of my mom's arms and grabbed each side of her to help her finish. Word got around fast that she was nearing the finish line, and we heard on the speaker, "Please don't leave yet! Angie is finishing the race! I repeat, Angie is finishing the race!"

She started chanting with everything left in her, "I will finish the race that is set before me! I will finish the race that is set before me!"

We looked up, and everyone in the race was crying and sprinting to run the last long stretch behind her. My dad and Gannon had their arms wide open for her at the finish line, and right before she crossed, she proclaimed, "This is my race, and I will finish it! God is my strength!"

She collapsed at the finish line and began throwing up, but she had made it. She had finished everything that she had started. This story runs through my head often, as this is a true example of who she was. God was her strength, and nothing was impossible in her eyes.

A few weeks later, she texted us to let us know she passed out on the floor, and that my dad found her and was taking her to the ER. There had been a lot of false alarms before like this, so we just kept thinking she'd live forever. When she was admitted to the hospital that day, Josh and I were still not back together, but oddly, he came to the house that night and silently laid next to me. He just asked if he could be there in the house with me. And this time, I said yes. We didn't say another word to one another, but Josh laid there and held me the whole night.

We forgot to lock the door of the house that night, and we woke up the next morning with my brother Zeke standing over us in bed. He told us we needed to get to the hospital right away. When we walked into her room, my mom sat up. She became consumed with talking about money and worrying about taking care of everyone. Things like keeping my dad out of debt and making sure her grandkids knew who she was were on her mind. My parents still lived in the same house that they had moved into when they adopted Mike. After his passing, they didn't want to leave, so they purchased the house. She really wanted this one last Christmas with her kids and grandkids.

When the doctor finally came in, he told us, "Here's the deal. I don't think your mom is going to live another week. This is her choice, but I can do another round of radiation, and it will either take her down fast or help her last maybe another two weeks at best." With Christmas and my dad's birthday right around the corner, we knew which choice she would make.

My mom said that she wanted her family to see that she did everything in her power to stay alive. After giving up all sugar, only drinking alkaline water, eating organic, working out, and always doing the recommended chemo and radiation, she wasn't about to give up now. As she was wheeled back for radiation, I texted MTV to let them know what was happening.

It's so upsetting that people think MTV used her death for ratings. They told us that they were going to respect our family, and they would stay out of it or film it, but it was up to my mom and all of us. From day one, they had nothing but respect for her.

"I'm sharing my life, and I can't just end my story. I need people to see the end of my life," my mom told the producer. She said that there was no reason to live life other than to be kind and help others. "It costs nothing to always be kind," she said. She wanted to share that one last time with the world, and she told them to fly out to film because she had a message to share with the world. Still to this day, I wonder what exactly that message would have been.

After that last round of chemotherapy, I just knew that she was going to make it, and likely, she'd stay alive even longer than we thought, because that's what always seemed to happen. I thought she would give a great message that MTV would film, and then we'd go about our lives getting ready for the holidays. My mom would be so thrilled that she could see her grandkids open presents. But, as God would have it, she came back to us nearly unresponsive. I kept waiting for her to wake up and walk out like the strong woman she was—just as she had when she got sick with pneumonia during her cancer journey and nearly died. One day, she just sat up, started talking, and worked her way back to health. Why couldn't she do that now? She often told us that she never wanted to be bedbound. "If I'm alive, I want to be alive and not in pain," she reminded us often. She also told us that never once was she scared to die because she knew exactly where she was going—with no more pain, suffering, or sin.

She was such a super woman. I thought the whole time she would jump up and say, "Okay, Brad. Take me home!" On day three, we were all sitting around her, singing and telling stories, and my dad calmly said that's when it really started to hit him that we were losing her.

My sister Whitney cried and told our mom how much she loved her. One by one, we all went up to say our goodbyes. Josh even went up and held her hand, cried, and thanked her for raising his son when he wasn't there. He thanked her for taking him in as her own and carrying us through everything. He was right. My mom had held our hands and helped us through so much.

So many people came in to see her, and at some point, it dawned on me. What my mom wanted more than anything before she passed was to have our house paid off so my dad would have no debt. If I could make this one last dream come true for her, I was going to do it, so I got online and made a fundraiser page for her. I asked people to give what they could, even if it was just fifty cents. I wanted one of her last memories to be feeling the weight lifted off her shoulders from the house being paid off. Thousands of people answered the call with fifty cents and one-dollar donations, and it added up, because she had over 100,000 followers on social media. Some, like MTV and some cast members, were so generous with us at that time, giving us thousands. Between the fundraiser and their generosity, we reached our goal.

She was still unconscious when we leaned down to tell her about the house, and we could hardly believe it when she finally opened her eyes and said, "What? I love you guys." She spent her whole life serving others, and people were finally paying her back. You could see so much stress leave her body. She had already paid nearly half of it off with a running fundraiser we had and all of her love offerings from her speaking engagements.

We were all scared to leave her side, so we got sitters for the kids and slept on the floor of her hospital room, with our spouses never leaving our sides. One night, as we all slept, I woke up for a minute and saw that Josh had chosen to stay up all night and just sit by her side. It was day four, and MTV and others had come together to feed us so we didn't have to leave. We were all standing around her with our hands on her body, singing her favorite songs to her.

My dad held his hand on her forehead while she took her last breath, and her sister Mandi Smith, who is also her best friend in life, said, "Cross the finish line, Angie!"

I remember hearing my sister Kaylee cry louder than I knew she could, and I said, "No, no! This isn't happening. This isn't real."

My best friend Cayla was there and stayed with me because she felt I needed her. Both she and Josh squeezed me with their hands as I shook. I put my head on my mom's leg and cried. I couldn't leave. I was paralyzed. Eventually, everyone else cleaned up the room and left, but Josh waited with me as I sat and stared for about an hour and kissed her forehead. She was always warm, but this time, she was cold. This was just her shell because she was in Heaven now, and I imagined her holding the hands of the two babies I had lost due to miscarriages and telling them about how much they are loved. It was one of the few things that gave me comfort in that moment. I also knew her adopted son Mike was waiting excitedly to hug her.

The only thing I remember about the drive home was the winding roads. I don't even remember walking into the house or how I told the kids. I was a walking zombie, and I thought I would hurt the most because she was my emotional support and the only one who believed in me no matter what mistakes I made. Josh and I slept in the living room that night with my dad. It hurt him too badly to go sleep in the bed they had shared. He was what hurt us kids the most. People were bringing food, gift baskets, and he was laying on the floor saying, "Angie, I need you. Come back!" He was so lonely, and I ended up moving in with him for a month after she passed, and Jaxie slept in the bed with him every night. I was so happy that my siblings and I came together to take care of my dad during that time.

I'm really proud of the way the town came together when my mom got sick. When she was in her last days and close to death, cars backed up for three blocks to pray around her house. Everyone who knew her was aware that she walked and prayed seven times around our house every single day since we lived there, no matter the weather. She prayed for our future spouses, even when we were kids. So, this time, people gathered around her little home to walk and pray. One final time, she was the shining light drawing people together in the name of God and love.

Crowning Achievement:

My mom fought the good fight, kept her faith, and finished her race across the finish line into Heaven. I am so thankful my mom loved God and was able to lead several people to the Lord through MTV and social media. I'm honored to tell her story and that our family gets to carry on her legacy.

Chapter 25

DON'T LET THE WORLD STOP YOU

For nothing will be impossible with God.
Luke 1:37

When my mom died, I completely lost it. I began projecting all of my anger on Josh—pushing him away, crying, and telling him he was awful. I had also gone on dating websites and started seeing someone else. I always hid from the camera when I was off seeing other men. Josh and I were off and on at that time—not really together but not completely apart. And to make matters worse, we were still filming with MTV, which made things pretty horrible with Josh.

One day, when I was on my way back from this guy's house and Josh was still living at home, I called him. He said, "Do you think we should just divorce?" I said yes and told him to be gone by the time I got home that night.

When I got home, he was slamming doors, yelling that he was done with me and MTV and that he would sign the papers and be gone so I could have freedom with this other man. Josh, too, had been living a separate life and going to another woman who I thought was my friend. She came over and explained that she was giving him advice and felt bad for the way I was treating him. She even showed me text messages where he had said he was only staying with me for the kids. He had told her that he just couldn't do this anymore because I pushed him away too much. This didn't hurt me because of Josh, but it did hurt because I thought I knew and could trust her. I forgive her in my heart, but I will never speak to her again.

Instead of staying quiet, though, I wrote a status update on Facebook about it, and it blew up. Of course, articles about Josh cheating with this woman popped up all over the internet. Again, I took Benadryl and drank during the day because I couldn't sleep or function. I was highly medicated on several depression medications. It had been months of being separated, and again, being alive was too much pain to handle. Josh would text here and there to catch up, but I'd just ignore him. We'd been together so long—grew up together, actually, and Josh loved me when I was *just Mackenzie*. Anyone else who would come after him would likely know "TV Mackenzie" instead, and I might not know if they loved me for who I truly was or for a shot to be on TV. I went through so many seasons of life with him that I would never experience with anyone else, but it was time to move on. People on the internet were right. It was toxic and time to go our separate ways. I had no love left in my heart for him—or anyone, for that matter. I just needed some way to crawl out of this hellhole.

I got an unexpected call one day during this time from my boss. I would often travel down to Florida to work with him and his fitness and nutrition company that I was a huge part of, but so far, most of my work had been done remotely from Oklahoma. This time, though, he asked me if I'd ever thought about moving to Florida to be closer to the business. At first, I thought he was joking when he asked if I'd consider moving there, but I realized he wasn't kidding at all. I laughed and said, "You are too funny!" I was not one to ever leave home. All I ever knew was small-town Miami, Oklahoma.

I certainly wanted a chance to start over and grow. Nothing except my family was keeping me in Oklahoma, and this would be a good way to get away from Josh. In bed that night, my mind raced as I realized that the worst thing that could happen is that I move there, don't like it, and move back. Since hitting rock bottom, again, I needed a change of scenery, and what better place than the Sunshine State! At first, I thought, *"No way,"* but then I realized, *"Why not?"* It's not as hard as people may think. You just find work and a place to rent before packing up and leaving. Life is too short not to try to chase your dreams.

The next morning, I looked online and saw a house that was already furnished. A friend agreed to rent my house while I lived down there, so I started making plans. On my days off, I started cleaning the house and throwing things out. All the clothes that the kids and I didn't need were donated to women's shelters and thrift stores.

MTV called because a new season of *Teen Mom OG* was about to begin filming, and Josh had refused to sign on. Then, as I was preparing to move, coronavirus struck, and I thought

MTV was going to call things off because of the pandemic. To my surprise, they said they would quarantine and live in Florida near me.

Now it was time to tell my family. They had a hard time seeing me in such a dark place, but they, too, were experiencing grief. Even so, they had rock-solid marriages, and I didn't, and they told me this sounded like a good opportunity and supported my decision. My friends told me this would be impossible and that their exes wouldn't dare allow them to move with their kids across the country.

Finally, it was time to tell Josh. Had the tables been turned, I would have thrown a fit and made sure he didn't leave. I mustered up the courage and said, "Josh, I got offered an opportunity to go to Florida and work."

Silence filled the room, and he softly replied. "Okay, I think this will be good for you, but don't forget that I am their dad." He agreed that we could work things out with the kids, and he could take them over summer and Christmas break, as well as visit us in Florida sometimes. I couldn't believe he was so accepting of this and wondered if he already had a girlfriend and was excited to have this chance to move on. Or was he just ready to see me happy after all this time? In the end, I didn't really care, since I was about to go live my best life yet.

A week before I moved, a girl reached out to Josh and said she had inappropriate photos of me. My ex had taken them and saved them on his phone. He was disgusted, and now I was the one making him look bad. He just wanted everything to be over. The producers approached Josh once more and said they wanted to give him a chance to tell his side of the story about what happened, since he was still all over the tabloids.

"There is a difference between her and me. I don't care what people think of me, and she does care what people think of her. She runs a business where people follow her and purchase her workout programs. I don't want to ruin her name or make her look bad. I just wish she would stop doing it to me," he said.

I honestly didn't even care at that point. We started packing, and I could see he was sad. The night before we left, he came over and helped us pack with one of my friends. Then, my friend moved all of her things into my house, and Josh just watched this all happen. He asked to just lay with me, like he did that night before my mom passed, and I'm not usually one to do something like that, but I did that night.

The next day as we were gearing up to leave, MTV wanted to film. Josh wanted to hug me goodbye, and it was a private moment because they couldn't film him. While holding me, he asked one more time, "Can we please start over and never talk about our problems again? I don't have any anger toward you." I didn't have much to say in the moment, and I told him I needed to get going because the kids were waiting in the car. As he stood on the porch and watched us drive off, a part of me wanted to get out of my car and run and grab him, but I needed to do this alone and learn to live life without him.

I drove by my dad's house and gave him a hug. Everyone was standing in his yard, saying their goodbyes. It was so hard, but I knew they were happy that I was taking a step to get myself out of the scary headspace I had been in.

On the way to Florida, I felt so powerful and happy that I was making this change for myself and the kids. I also knew this was going to be a great season on *Teen Mom OG*, as it would show the growth and changes I was making. Josh called several times to check on us while we were on the road, and at one point,

Gannon said to me, "You know you can't take our dad from us, right? We still love him." That was a tough moment—like being punched in the gut. I assured him that his dad would still be very much in his life.

Crowning Achievement:

As I'm writing this book, I have now lived in Florida for half a year. I don't know what my future holds, but I can say that I challenge everyone to leave their hometowns and live somewhere else at least once. It has opened up so many doors, and my eyes have seen a whole new world. I have met amazing friends, and I'm in a spot where businesses thrive. I love being around different cultures and diversity. I love the beaches, sunshine, and palm trees, and I can honestly say I'm happy. I feel like the sky's the limit, and I can run as far as my heart desires. I know my mom would be proud.

Chapter 26

REMEMBER WHOSE DAUGHTER YOU ARE AND STRAIGHTEN YOUR CROWN

*Anyone you forgive, I also forgive. And what I have
forgiven—if there was anything to forgive—I have
forgiven in the sight of Christ for your sake.*
2 Corinthians 2:10

've been in Florida now for over six months. After about a
month of living apart, Josh came down to visit, and shortly
after, he moved all of his things down to live with us. I think
the move helped us both realize that we just want our family
back. I began to miss his warm hugs that made me feel at home,
and the kids were dying to see him again. However, I followed
his lead. I never called or texted first. I knew if we were meant
to divorce, it would happen peacefully. And if we were meant

to be, he would find a way to be with his family eighteen hours away. And he did.

I think grief and some of Josh's choices changed me forever, and then when I lost my mom, I also lost a huge part of myself. My family, especially my dad, will never be the same. I've grown to be more humble, but I also have some walls up. I don't let Josh in the way that I used to, but I don't think either Josh or I are bad people or serial cheaters the way the internet portrays us. I do, however, think we married and had kids way too young without knowing what we even wanted in life as individuals, and that made life hard.

I try to be the best mom I can be, and I must admit that the kids are so much happier now that Josh is here. We do something as a family every week and have a lot of fun together. We haven't really fought since he's been here.

I don't let him see me cry or see my pain, and I don't know if he carries pain because of the things I've done to him. I would never know, because while I carry my emotions right up front for everyone to see, he immediately forgives me and hides his feelings deep down. It's been a rough road to recovering from life. I understand that many people don't like our love story, and believe me, I wanted this book to be a redemption story with a "happily ever after" ending. On the other hand, some people love that we haven't given up and we've made it this long.

Life hit me hard when I couldn't call my mom for advice anymore. She was the glue that held me together. I never really leaned on Josh. I loved him but always went to my mom. It was like the three of us were in a marriage together, and now I have to learn to just be with Josh. To make this work, we're going to have to find some strong glue.

A lot of people say that I must feel forced to stay with Josh because God would see it as a sin to divorce, but it has nothing to do with my religion or relationship with God. We just always find our way back to one another in the end. Josh holds a special place in my heart and always will no matter what ends up happening. If we divorce, that's okay, and he's still my good friend. He is still the one I grew up with and made several life mistakes with. What is shown on TV now is what our true relationship looks like. Some people ask how I had the strength to fight so hard to make it work, but that's simply not the truth. I gave up and walked away, and that's the best advice I could give anyone. Don't fight for anything—let it go and let it fall into place how it should be. Josh is not responsible for my happiness. I am. And if we continue to depend on another human to make us happy, we will continue to be disappointed. It was me who needed to change, and I have noticed it inspires him to be better. There is a famous quote attributed to Maya Angelou that says a woman's heart should be so hidden in God that a man has to seek Him just to find her. That is where I was in life. I was growing spiritually, and Josh was going to have to turn to God to find me again. Ladies, let your man go. Cling to God, and He will show you the answers. Don't force your own storyline.

For the longest time, I was a very unhappy person. I was so full of hate and resentment, and I wanted to feel human again. Living in resentment made me feel like I was driving down the road and my car had run out of gas. It is my own fault for forgetting to fill my tank up. I was stuck on the side of the road, but the rest of the cars were moving forward in life, driving past me. The world still spins and doesn't stop for anyone. When I was stuck in a dark place, I couldn't see the blessings God had for me, and

I couldn't even celebrate what God was doing for others, because I was still stuck on the side of the road.

After my move to Florida, I regained my relationship with God and got off of my medication, which meant I was now experiencing raw feelings again and working through them. I know time will be healing. When I struggled with forgiveness, God helped me see all the things he has forgiven me for as well as the things Josh and my mom have. When I was refusing to forgive people for doing me wrong, not only was it selfish, but it was like waking up every morning, drinking poison, and expecting the other person to die. But I was the one who was suffering, and I choose to forgive, not because I am weak, but for my own happiness.

I have learned that marriage is a journey. If my story would have turned out the way I wanted, I would be rich, perfect, smart, and no one would have ever done me wrong. But this is the beauty of life. Our journeys make us who we become in the end. We have a choice to turn our pain into bad or good. A true queen isn't one who lives a perfect life; she's one who has battles thrown her way and is still able to get up, put her best foot forward, and straighten her crown.

On hard days, I say to myself: "*Whenever you feel overwhelmed, remember whose daughter you are and straighten your crown.*"

My mom was a true queen. Nothing stopped her from becoming who she wanted to become and achieving what was on her mind. I have a text on my phone, the last text she ever sent me, that was a reply to me asking her if she is going to be okay. That text says, "I will be just fine; I'm a warrior."

She always called me a warrior too. Any time I'd get knocked down in life, instead of babying me, she would look at me and remind me that I was a warrior and that I would overcome what I was facing.

She reminded me so many times that last year of her life that she always knew I'd go far in life. She said how proud she was of me for picking up two small items and opening what has become a four-year-strong successful business where I have now employed my siblings too. She had a lot of good talks with her kids while she was sick. We all have our own stories, but one vivid talk she had with me that I think of daily was one where she called to tell me that God had spoken to her. She had reached hundreds of thousands of lives through her sickness, if not millions, and God told her she had done her work and that I was now going to carry on her legacy and reach people. I don't know for sure, but maybe being vulnerable and sharing my raw truth in this book was what God was talking to her about.

The beauty of opening up is that people start telling you stories and sharing about themselves. Telling my story and hearing from others has been therapeutic for me. Although some see me, my family, and my mistakes as simply entertainment on TV or as food for tabloid gossip, I'm a human, a resilient overcomer who may be wired differently than others, but who just wants to be the best version of myself I can be—for myself, but more importantly, for my children and family. My daughter and two sons may not be old enough to go through the same kind of heartbreaks that I have, but I'm going to raise them with love, courage, compassion, and strength so they can't be broken. Now that this queen has been working to straighten her crown, she can help her little princes and princess to straighten theirs. And just as my mom did, I will live life being a fighter until my very last breath on Earth.

Crowning Achievement:

Every day we wake up with a choice to grow. Today, tomorrow, and the next, I choose to continue to be a warrior, to straighten my crown, and to make my momma proud like the warrior she always told me I was.

ABOUT THE AUTHOR

Mackenzie Douthit McKee starred on the MTV reality TV shows *16 & Pregnant* and *Teen Mom 3*, and she currently appears on *Teen Mom OG*. She has become a fan favorite for sharing the ups and downs of her life with the world, as well as her love of family and God. Mackenzie's determination and drive has led to her success as the creator and owner of BodyByMac, a fitness company that aims to help others meet their health

Author photo credit: Whitney Osborn

and wellness goals. In addition to being a mother of three, she is also a popular social media personality and influencer. She has homes in both Oklahoma and Florida, which she shares with her husband, Josh McKee, and their children.

Julie Markussen is a lifelong lover of nonfiction books and a reality TV junkie. She has been referenced in several books and academic journals for her essays on the music of Elvis Presley. Originally from Iowa, she now lives in California. She is a lover of American pop culture, vintage paper dolls, and classic Hollywood movies.

ACKNOWLEDGMENTS

Thank you to my ghostwriter, Julie Markussen. Getting the right person to write with is super important…a make or break deal. You made it comfortable to open up and share some really raw things about my life. Thanks for pushing me out of my comfort zone to do this dang thing.